DECODING
YOUR
TEENAGER

DECODING

· · · · *YOUR* · · · ·

TEENAGER

How to Understand Each Other During the Turbulent Years

Michael DeSisto

WILLIAM MORROW AND COMPANY, INC.

New York

Recognizing the importance of perserving what has been written, it is the policy of William Morrow and Company, Inc., and its imprints and affiliates to have the books it publishes printed on acid-free paper, and we exert our best efforts to that end.

Library of Congress Cataloging-in-Publication Data
DeSisto, A. Michael.
  Decoding your teenager : how to understand each other during the turbulent years / A. Michael DeSisto.
    p. cm.
  ISBN 0-688-08776-0
  1. Parenting—United States. 2. Communication in the family—United States. 3. Parent and child—United States. 4. Adolescent psychology—United States. I. Title
HQ755.85.D47   1991
306.874—dc20   90-41532
                                                                    CIP

Printed in the United States of America

First Edition

1 2 3 4 5 6 7 8 9 10

BOOK DESIGN BY ROBIN MALKIN

For Margie Charles—the wife

ACKNOWLEDGMENTS

First, there was Miss Hurdy; she was the first grade teacher. I remember I used to sit on the curbstone in front of her house in the afternoon, waiting for her to come home. Or I would ride my bike near her house, so she would go by, and say "Hi" . . . a "Hi" from her meant so much. But then there were many others: There was Sister Eudes and Sister Theophane and Miss Quane . . .

In college, there was the college, *The College*. Stonehill College, the college that gave me the break, that gave me time, that gave me space. There was Mr. Dillon and Mr. Cleary and Mr. Fraser and Brassil Fitzgerald and Mr. Dillon and Mr. Dillon and Mr. Dillon.

The hardest part of life for all of us is finding people we need: I was very fortunate to have many people there many times to give me the things that I needed. There was Herman Baker, who gave me books, who gave me friendship, who gave me fathering. There were Peg and Laurie Lodge, who provided another family for me and ideas I had never had before. Then, of course, there are Deb and Uncle Mil, the in-laws for whom the fictional prenuptial agreement gives me custody.

And there was Al Brayson, who trusted me; Helen Hafner, who loved and mentored me; Elsie and Kinderland, who nurtured me; Elaine Goldman Jacks, who believed in me; and Thomas Duncan, who risked with me, as well as Will Roberts, Joe Papp, Ted Mann, Sy Winn, Gerry Abraham, and Erma Brode, and all the parents who financially supported my beginning my own school. And then there are all the children I've ever known who have trusted me enough to let me touch them, who allowed themselves to be vulnerable, and who allowed me to walk with them to a new place. And the ones who adopted me: Scott and Stefan and Mark and Marie.

And there were Jim and Alan and Johanna, and I musn't forget Stanley, and most recently, John, for helping me make sense out of the often senseless. And then there is the staff who learned from me, resisted me, and supported me, and there was August who let me love him. And then there is my best friend Bobby, my best friend Joe, and my best friend Bunny. And then there is Amy—Amy the sage, Amy the carer, Amy the understander, Amy who keeps my days together. And then there's Bill Proctor, the scribe, the friend, the lover of mankind.

My eternal thanks to my tireless mother who worked, and fought, and deluged me with all the love and caring of which she was capable; and to Jacque, my sister, alias John Smith, the student, the altar boy, the actress, the singer, the friend, the person for whom I cooked, the person I teased, the person I love; and to Elaine, and the nephews Joseph, Stephen, Peter and Michael who—I try to make proud of me.

To all of you who have given me so much I profoundly put my hands together and bow my head and both acknowledge and thank. And to those of you who, in my humanness and frailty I have forgotten to mention, I do so in spirit. And to the Higher Power on which, I believe, we all in some way depend, I thank you.

CONTENTS

PART I

The Secret to Talking with Your Teenager

CHAPTER 1

The Birth of a Real *Talking Relationship*

A real talking relationship with a teenager always begins with caring—and is consummated through an unswerving parental commitment to break through, whatever the personal effort or cost.

I learned about caring and also about getting through to difficult people at an early age. It all began with my father, who died when I was only eleven. Despite the brief time I was able to spend with him, the way he dealt with people made an indelible impression on me.

My dad was a contractor whose company did a lot of hard pick-and-shovel roadwork. In many such companies, the employees *hate* their jobs. They can't wait to move on to something else. But not those who worked for Mr. DeSisto.

You see, my dad really cared for his workers, and he showed his concern in many small but significant ways. For example, he knew how physically demanding a laborer's job was, and so he arranged to transport his employees to and from the job sites. He didn't want them dissipating their energies or wasting their money on commuting.

Also, he never fired anybody. When a man would get too elderly or infirm to wield his tools effectively on the roads, my father would move him into a less tiring job, such as lawn work. Many times, he'd actually *create* a job, just so the older worker would have a place to spend his final working years in productivity and dignity.

He was always remembering them and their families in small ways, such as by sending flowers. I became so accustomed to seeing carnations, tulips, or roses sent out to friends and co-workers, that I came to accept this practice simply as something that a polite, civilized person did. In fact, I picked up the habit myself after I reached adulthood.

The impact of this sort of caring emerged clearly over the years as so many of his people continued to work for him up to the age of retirement. Not only that, they reciprocated his caring attitude by bringing him such gifts as they could afford. Hardly a weekend went by without our receiving vegetables from their home gardens, an embroidered piece of linen, or some other token of their appreciation.

But their feelings came across perhaps most clearly when Dad died. I can still remember arriving at the funeral parlor in 1951 and seeing dozens of his old Italian laborers sitting outside the building. Many of them were crying, they were so upset at his passing.

My father never said to me in so many words, "It's important for you to care for others." But the message came across clearly in the way he lived and related to others.

Also, the emphasis on being a caretaker for others was reinforced in my relationship with my mother. Beginning when I was just a young child, she was very dependent on me, always insisting that I be available to run errands or just to provide moral support. I cared for her in a variety of ways—but more caring always seemed to be required. In fact, her reliance on me often left me with the impression that nothing I could do for her would ever be enough.

Clearly, my mother went too far in her demands. But more often than not, when parents become excessive, overbearing, or otherwise unwise in dealing with their kids, the kids respond by becoming stronger or developing skills that would have been impossible with moms or dads who are "normal" or "well balanced." In other words, a parent's mistakes, excesses, shortcomings, or pathology can actually work in a child's favor.

In a variety of different ways, then, I know that the attitudes and values espoused and promoted by my parents were communicated in a powerful way to me. The final result? Now I place caring for others—and especially the teenagers under my care—at the top of my list of priorities. In fact, my whole life has been devoted to the role of caretaker!

This caring impulse became apparent as soon as I left home for college and graduate school: I chose to be trained as a teacher and counselor. Also, I spent years working with kids in various classrooms. Finally, during the past decade, I've founded and operated a boarding school—the DeSisto Schools in Stockbridge, Massachusetts.

In my work with students, I suppose I've encountered almost every teenage problem imaginable, from promiscuous sex, to explosive anger and violence, to drug abuse, to chronic "runaway-itis," to destructive overachievement. Clearly, my early childhood influences have come into full bloom in the adult years. By most outward indications, I would now have to be regarded as a proven, seasoned caretaker of teenage children—a development for which both my parents are responsible.

But caring is only the beginning.

As I've already suggested, it's also necessary to find ways to *break through* a child's defenses. Only when all the obstacles to intimate talk have been stripped away will you be free to express your care and concern fully.

Again, let me return to a personal example. As a schoolboy, I was frequently victimized by other children. I was a relatively small kid, and I didn't like to fight—a formula that was ready-made to attract every bully in hailing distance.

To compensate for my vulnerability, I learned at an early age to read the minds and motives of difficult and dangerous people. It was a matter of survival. If I could figure out what factors drove a bully, I knew I'd have a better chance to take steps to avoid his wrath, or perhaps manipulate him or even make friends with him. Then, I figured, I'd have a better chance of staying safe and unscarred.

Unfortunately, this story doesn't have a classic Hollywood happy ending. Recess remained a time of high anxiety for me, as I continued to be beaten and pushed around more than I would have liked. But at least I eventually came to understand how to minimize the violence.

Also, I picked up important information for the future: The lessons I learned greatly strengthened my hand in dealing with teenagers as a professional teacher, counselor, and headmaster —and as a parent.

Although my wife and I don't have any children of our own, we adopted a teenager, a boy by the name of Scott, who had run away from home. He's in his mid-twenties now, having passed through the trials and tribulations of adolescence years ago. But I wouldn't trade anything for what Scott taught me during those turbulent teenage years when he was under my care: I'm sure I was the main beneficiary as I observed at close hand, on a day-to-day basis in my own home, the way the principles I'll be discussing in this book work in a real-life family situation.

To sum up, then, two traits are absolutely essential in those who hope to learn to talk with difficult children:
      1) the ability first to care deeply; and
      2) the ability to break through.

In the following pages, I'll be sharing many experiences and insights with you in the hope that you'll be able to glean some guidelines for caring deeply and breaking through successfully to your own teenager.

Among other things, we'll discuss:

- How to cope with your own "benephobia," my term for parents' inability to enjoy their teenager
- How to identify your teenager's "Kid Type"—i.e., your child's particular, overriding set of traits and problems
- Practical and proven responses to such major teenage challenges as peer relationships, drugs, sexual development, abuse, anger, and the pressure to achieve
- The concept of understanding and drawing up "job descriptions" for parents and teens
- Rules and strategies for playing the all-important "family games" that shape your relationship with your child
- The best uses of power in parent-child interactions
- The exercise of courage in family confrontations
- Suggestions for avoiding the "Sieve Syndrome" (defined as an inability to be filled up or satisfied by personal relationships or by other good things in life)
- How to manage teenage anger
- Escape routes from the "money muddles" that taint many parent-teen relationships
- The true meaning of the "I" word, "intimacy"
- The role of intuition in dealing with teens

- Practical approaches to improving the level of trust in your family
- Ways to identify the natural pace of change in your adolescent's development
- Special considerations that parents should keep in mind in dealing with a teenager of the same or different sex
- How to develop appropriate outlets for expressing "not-OK" feelings
- The role of the hug, pat, or kiss in parent-teen encounters
- How to make your shortcomings as a parent work *for* your teenager
- Some basic parental responses to the problem of addiction
- Suggestions for eliminating the blaming, finger-pointing element from child-rearing

Over the years, in my responsibilities as teacher, counselor, and headmaster, I've worked with thousands of teenagers—many of them classic "problem children" from upscale homes. As they have confronted me with agonizing decisions and tough questions on sex, drugs, money troubles, and the meaning of life, I've often been pushed to my emotional and professional limits. Yet, these kids have been my teachers as well as my students.

On one level, having to respond to them and try to help them work through their problems has forced me to fine-tune my approach as a counselor and therapist. But just as important, I've also learned something about becoming the teenager's *friend*.

For the most part, my students seem to feel free to walk in and out of my home, which is situated in the middle of one of the campuses, and share their problems, frustrations, and joys. During these interchanges, though I'm supposed to be the "wise counselor,'' I often find that I'm as much the beneficiary and learner as they are.

These school-related experiences—along with personal insights I've gained as a father *and* son—have taught me that it is indeed possible to succeed as the parent of teenagers. It's also possible to talk openly and freely with them—*if* you take some time first to try to understand how they think and feel.

But first, it's essential to take a few moments to look inside yourself. In particular, let's examine more closely the personal feelings and family baggage that may be impeding your ability to communicate fully with your teenager.

CHAPTER 2

Understanding Your Basic Dilemma as a Parent

If you're like most parents, the major dilemma you face as a mother or father is that you don't really know how to enjoy your teenager. Consider for a moment the flux of feelings you've felt about your teenager during the past couple of days. Some possibilities:

- You worry about his grades.
- You agonize over the possibility that he may use drugs.
- She frustrates you because of the boys she dates—and the sexual activity you suspect she's engaged in.
- You argue with your child far too often.
- You're confused about how to be an effective parent of a teenager.
- You feel inadequate in trying to come up with a plan that will put your child on the right track in life. (Even more depressing, you suspect that even if you *do* come up with the perfect plan, your child will refuse to follow it!)

- You sometimes feel like a stranger in dealing with your kids: You don't know what to say to them—and they don't seem to care about relating to you.
- You periodically feel like a complete failure as a parent.
- You don't seem to be able to impress your child with the basic principles and values of life that you know are essential for happiness and success.
- Sometimes—or perhaps *many* times—you find yourself sighing or shaking your head because your youngster's performance or behavior has fallen short of your expectations.

Once the teenage years arrive, parental controls slip away, and old sanctions that once constrained unacceptable behavior no longer work. This loss of control leads to agony and pain in a parent's encounters with a child.

Sometimes, there may even be a feeling of fear. After all, he marches to a different drummer than you do. So on occasion, you may become afraid that the beat he hears will lead him down a destructive path to drugs, promiscuous sex, or even crime and violence.

With such anxieties and nagging concerns upsetting their emotional equilibrium, few mothers and fathers these days find that they can sit back and really *savor* and *enjoy* a teenager's presence and special personality.

When a child is quite young, parents may experience rather lengthy periods of uninterrupted joy—such as witnessing the first few steps, or listening to the first words, or watching a toddler laugh or express naive wonder at an otherwise ordinary event, like the falling of a leaf or the play of sunlight on a roof.

Of course, young children can also provide plenty of frustrations, along with the joys. What parent, for instance, hasn't lost sleep responding to a cranky two- or three-year-old? What big-city yuppie hasn't agonized about whether a preschooler is going to be admitted into a certain nursery school or kindergarten? What parent in any generation has avoided periodic terror in the face of one of those inevitable childhood injuries?

On the whole, however, the earliest years seem to produce more happiness and contentment than concern. In contrast, as a boy or girl gets older, the worries tend to outweigh the joy and wonder.

Questions I hear all the time from parents of teenagers run the gamut of academic and social concerns:

"Why isn't his math progressing as well as we had hoped?"

"Is that score on her aptitude tests high enough?"

"Why wasn't she invited to Lisa's party?"

"What can I do to relieve his depression, now that he didn't make the cut for the soccer team?"

"Is he being exposed to drugs at school?"

"Is she engaging in sex with her boyfriend?"

These kinds of questions are certainly pressing and important. But I don't believe they are the best place to begin if you hope to improve your relationship and get on real talking terms with your teenager.

A more promising first step would be to take a good, close look at yourself and ask, "Why can't I *enjoy* my teenager more?"

The most likely answer: As the parent of a teenager, you probably have a case of benephobia.

WHAT IS BENEPHOBIA?

During the decades I've spent counseling and observing teenage children and their parents, I've stumbled upon a few truths about human relationships that I believe to be absolute. One of these involves what I call *benephobia*.

Simply put, benephobia is a word I've coined which refers to the fear of feeling well, good, or happy. Without exception, everyone I know—even those who consider themselves "well adjusted" or "emotionally healthy"—suffers from this malady.

To understand how benephobia works in a person's life—and how it can influence those around him—consider this experience I had as "Smokey the Bear":

More than twenty years ago, I worked in a camp for inner-city kids, and during my tenure, I developed a persona called "Smokey the Bear." My job was to serve as a kind of ranger out in the woods. I taught the kids, who were mostly of elementary school age, how to cook, forage, and survive in the forest.

During the months I had this job, I wore a uniform consisting of chinos and a rough old shirt, and I also grew a beard. The children, who would be brought out to me by their counselors, viewed me with a kind of awe because as this Smokey the Bear character, I was seen as being a little more than human. I had all the answers about the woods, and every kid, without exception, wanted to be my special friend and seemed willing to believe or follow anything I said.

In some ways, this was the best job I ever had in my whole life. I truly loved what I was doing, and everybody—including the kids, the other counselors, and the director of the camp—loved me. It was an unconditional love, one with no strings attached. It seemed that I could do no wrong.

But then, a strange thing happened. Somehow, I found I couldn't quite stand all the adulation and happiness. I wasn't used to being accepted totally, without any reservations. In the past, even when I had done quite well, there were always qualifications:

"Michael, you did a good job here, *but . . .*"

Or, "Hey, that was a nice piece of work! In the future, though . . ."

Or, "An excellent performance! Now, let me make some suggestions for improvement . . ."

With this camp, however, there was only praise. Only acceptance. Only love.

And frankly, I couldn't stand it.

It's hard to explain my deepest inner responses, except to say that I was *afraid* of feeling too good, and as a result, the praise made me nervous.

Sometimes, I thought, "These people don't really know me. What's going to happen when they find out who or what I *really* am?"

Other times I worried, "I'm bound to trip up before long. Things can't go on being this great forever. The ax is going to fall!"

Or I'd start thinking, "Maybe I shouldn't be working at a place like this, if they have so little discernment about people. Probably I should move on to a job where the people can understand me for what I really am."

Eventually, I became so rattled that I actually began making plans to leave the camp. Predictably, I seized on an otherwise manageable incident to precipitate a crisis and make my exit: One of the children wet the bed, and a counselor made him wear a sign saying, "I wet the bed."

That enraged me, because I knew that making such a spectacle of the child was a bad way to handle the problem. Also, I was especially sensitive because I myself had had a bed-wetting problem as a youngster.

But those were just excuses to justify my departure. Really, the *main* reason I left that camp was that I couldn't stand being so happy and accepted!

I suspect that given my good standing there, if I had raised an objection to the treatment of that boy, the manner of dealing with bedwetting would have been changed. I was in a strong position to pressure the counselors and administration to lay down policies against embarrassing children unnecessarily.

But at that stage of my life, I wasn't in the mood for negotiation or social reform. I just wanted to get away from all those good feelings as fast as possible. In short, I had a *severe* case of benephobia! Because of my deep-rooted fear of personal happiness, I was incapable of enjoying myself to the fullest in my interactions with other adults and with the children under my care.

I've found that the same kind of attitude obstructs the ability of *most* parents to engage in intimate, life-changing communication with their teenagers. Most mothers and fathers, either consciously or subconsciously, resist the notion that they are good parents. No matter how well they may seem to be doing to an outside observer, these parents, to one degree or another, see themselves as failures. Even when something great happens with their children, they fail to accept it completely or revel in it.

What's happening here?

Through the operation of a peculiar form of parental benephobia, these moms and dads have become fearful and doubtful about their ability to handle intense positive feelings about their family achievements. Instead, they find means to explain away their successes. Or they deny them—with the result that their children also begin to feel inadequate and shortchanged.

HOW BENEPHOBIC ARE YOU?

To understand better how the destructive forces of benephobia may work in your relationship with your child, reflect for a moment on your basic outlook on life and your aspirations for the future.

A major goal of most people—in many cases it's the person's *only* goal—is to be as happy as possible. Yet consistent, supreme happiness often seems an ephemeral, unachievable objective. In fact, we all live in a delicate balance between suicide and joy. Certain forces tug us down when we start feeling too good, just as another set of influences begins to bolster us up when we're feeling bad.

Understanding why these limits to happiness exist in your own life—and also how they may be caused to move upward or downward—is the first important secret you need to know about improving your relationship with your adolescent.

Although you want to be happy with your child, at some deep level, you're fearful of experiencing too much happiness. Yet, that fear—that benephobia—isn't set in stone. It can be reduced or even eliminated, once you identify the forces in yourself that tend to undercut or taint the joys of life.

To grasp this concept, it's helpful to picture your inner state of well-being as a parent on a graph, with total depression at the lower end of the scale, and unbounded joie de vivre at the upper end. When I'm discussing this concept, I usually draw a picture that looks something like this:

BENEPHOBIA SCALE

TOTAL JOY

(BENEPHOBIC ZONE)
COMFORT ZONE
(MALEPHOBIC ZONE)

SUICIDE

The only place a person can really feel good or "right" is in that narrow band on the scale that I've labeled *Comfort Zone*.

At first, you might assume that the happier or more joyous you become, the better you'll feel. But that's not necessarily so. Ironically, when your life becomes too happy—i.e., when you move *above* your comfort zone—there's a sense of feeling *too* good. This is the point at which benephobia takes over. Through a variety of inner mechanisms, a fear of feeling too good drives you back down to your most comfortable level.

My experience as Smokey the Bear is an example of how this odd phenomenon can work. I began to feel too wonderful and praised and accepted, and as a result, I started to look for ways to escape those feelings. My solution: to quit my job.

Just from my personal illustration, you've probably already noticed that not all comfort zones are the same. You, for instance, might have reacted quite differently at that camp from the way that I did. Perhaps your response to my story about Smokey may have gone something like this:

"DeSisto was all wrong! I'd *never* have felt uncomfortable

in that situation! All that positive feedback would have made me feel great!''

Maybe so. But believe me, you *do* have a comfort zone, even though it may be positioned a little differently from mine.

Also, there's no doubt that when certain experiences or feelings move you *above* that comfort zone, you automatically begin to feel a need to move yourself back down to more familiar—and comfortable—emotional territory.

The same mechanism can work in the opposite direction on the Benephobia Scale. We all know there are many "down" times in our lives—tragic events, failures, or uncontrollable negative feelings that inexorably pull us down below our comfort zone, into what I've called the *Malephobic Zone*.

When that happens, another set of uncomfortable feelings comes into play. But this time, the inner voice tells you, "I feel worse than I should feel or than I want to feel. So I have to take steps to move back up into my comfort zone."

How do you get back up to your accustomed comfort zone? There are countless possibilities. The most constructive ways may include seeking out supportive, positive friends, or perhaps a therapist. Or playing a favorite sport or game. Or listening to music. Or reading inspirational literature, or praying, or meditating.

Other, more destructive ways of escaping the malephobic zone include alcohol, drugs, promiscuous sex, or running away from the problems you face.

As many teenagers *and* adults know, these responses may temporarily make a person feel good. There may even be an illusion of moving back into the comfort zone or even above it. But it's only an illusion. When the effect of the transient "fix" wears off, the result will often be an emotional crash that drives the person even deeper into the malephobic zone—perhaps to the depths of despondency, and even to suicide.

* * *

With this introduction to the various zones on the Benephobia Scale, you now should be in a better position to evaluate some of the ways that you respond to the possibility of happiness or sadness in your relationship with your teenager.

But I'm not just interested in helping you understand where you are; more important, I want you to set a course that will significantly increase the level of satisfaction you experience with your teenager. And as you raise your comfort zone in this relationship, you'll find that talking with your child about things that really matter becomes much easier.

HOW TO RAISE YOUR COMFORT ZONE AS A PARENT

The quality of conversation you're able to have with your teenager is a direct barometer of how much you're able to enjoy the child. Typically, a low level of happiness in a relationship—a low comfort zone—is signaled by inane or nonexistent talk. So at the outset, I want you to focus on how well you communicate with your son or daughter.

First of all, you must recognize that you probably don't really feel all that comfortable talking to your adolescent child about certain tough or touchy issues—even though those topics may concern your child deeply.

Perhaps you begin to squirm a little when the talk about sex or dating habits gets too detailed. Or maybe you really don't want to know that your child is experimenting with drugs—you make an implicit assumption that ignorance is bliss!

As for your son's doubts about his academic abilities, or your daughter's fears about social acceptance, you'd prefer to postpone those discussions. You may feel you just don't have adequate answers, or you hope that if you ignore these adolescent concerns, they'll go away. In any event, if they don't disappear, there's always the hope that your child will learn to deal with them on his own!

Such parental escapism and denial usually reflect an unwillingness to move up from a familiar old comfort zone to a new level—a level that initially may produce feelings of discomfort, but in the end can usher in much more happiness, joy, and satisfaction. In other words, your benephobia is probably getting in the way of your ability to understand and influence your child. It's causing you to postpone or avoid completely the kind of straight, open talk that's essential to any mature relationship.

So what can you do about this problem?

To break out of the shackles of your present comfort zone as a parent—and to increase your capacity for genuine enjoyment and dialogue with your child—I'd suggest that you first look at yourself with a hard, realistic eye. The time has come for you to see just what kind of parent you really are.

SOME TYPICAL PARENTS

To help you in your self-analysis, I've described below a few typical kinds of parents that I've encountered over the years. These are all people with some serious limitation or block in their ability to enjoy their child and communicate fully with him.

You may or may not feel you fit precisely into any of these categories, but that's not the most important thing. Rather, you should allow these descriptions to trigger some serious thinking about who you are as a parent. Then, when you know yourself better, you'll be in a position to determine what you need to adjust in your own behavior to make it easier for you to get through to your child.

The Impatient Parent

It's easy to become so impatient that you focus on your teenager's flaws and failures rather than his progress. In this regard, I'm reminded of Will, a teenage boy I worked with over a period of nearly three years.

By some measures, Will didn't make much progress in his emotional development during his exposure to us. At the beginning of his stay at school, he had been unable to relate to women, except to get involved with a series of girls in promiscuous sexual liaisons. He couldn't carry on a serious conversation with an adult or teenage female, nor did he have the capacity to show real affection or love.

What were we able to do for Will? After the three years were over, I noticed that he was still enmeshed in the same problems that had plagued him when we had initially met. He still had trouble talking to girls, and he still got involved in ill-advised sexual encounters. So by one measure, you might say that neither we nor Will had done too well.

On the up side, however, Will had finally begun to recognize that he had a fundamental problem relating to women, and he was trying to deal with it. In an early encounter, he had looked at me vacantly when I tried to explain what he was doing. But now, after *years* of conversations, interactions, and therapy, a light was beginning to dawn.

For one thing, he saw that there was a connection between his unhappy home life and his present behavior toward women. His father had left home when he was quite young, and so he had not had any strong male role models to demonstrate how he could interact with a girl, other than through casual sex.

Also, his relationship with his mother had influenced his present behavior: He got along with her best when he was passive.

When he tried to assert himself or confront her, she responded violently and made life miserable for him. So he gave up trying to shape the interactions with his parent and allowed her to take the lead.

Predictably, that was also the way he related to the teenage girls in his life. He was drawn to those who actively seduced him, because that meant he could enter the relationship passively and avoid taking any initiative.

These were the factors that had influenced Will's attitudes and actions when I had first met him, and they *continued* to exert a powerful influence. But there was an interesting difference between the Will of three years ago and the Will of today: Before, he was more or less the unconscious pawn of the various forces in his family background. But now, he understood why he acted and reacted as he did—and he was taking steps to do something about it.

As for me, I could have deprecated the progress Will had made by saying, "Why couldn't he have moved along faster? Here it is, nearly three years since I first met him, and his forward movement has been extremely limited. He's *still* trying to get out of these promiscuous relationships!"

If I had chosen to have such an attitude, I would in effect have been saying, "I'm a lousy counselor, headmaster, and surrogate parent! I've let this boy down. He should be much further along than he is now."

Taking this tack would have made me feel limited and rather inadequate in my work and would have ensured that my own comfort zone remained down at the lower end of the scale. It would have been virtually impossible for me to enjoy this boy, much less engage him in a productive conversation.

But instead, I chose a more upbeat, less benephobic—and, I might add, more realistic—approach.

I said to myself, "Hey, I love this kid, and I've had a lot of fun getting to know him and helping him. Emotionally speaking, he's light-years ahead of where he was when he first came to me. Now he understands he has a problem, and he's developing the means to deal with it. He can actually *talk* with me about his difficulties! Not only that, he's actively trying to establish better relationships with the girls in his life."

I knew that this boy would probably be wrestling with his girl problems for years to come, but that was OK. That was to be expected. Those with deep-rooted emotional problems must often devote many years to working through their difficulties. The most I could expect to do was provide him with the tools to change his life, and that objective had been accomplished—in less than three years!

The moral to this story? Take the long view in your relationship with your child. Don't let your need for instant success or results get in the way of your acceptance or enjoyment of the *process* of development.

All personality changes are slow, like the change of direction of a large ocean liner. You can't turn your life around on a dime, you can't transform your deepest rooted habits overnight—and you certainly can't expect your teenager to achieve instantaneous, miraculous personal changes either.

In Will's case, the main signal that beneficial change was taking place was his ability to talk more freely with me, his surrogate parent. Watch for similar signals with your own teenager.

The Peak-Performance Parent

A high school sophomore named Jennifer, the oldest child in one West Coast family, was a top achiever in both her academic work and in sports. But no matter what Jennifer did—no matter what heights of accomplishment she reached—her mother and father would almost always echo (sometimes in unison!) a variation on this response: "Don't get complacent!"

These parents were typical of many mothers and fathers I've encountered who are extremely ambitious for their children. Because the mother and father were always pressing forward and setting goals for her, Jennifer never sensed she had won her parents' complete, unconditional approval.

Instead, Mom and Dad brushed the girl's successes aside and directed her toward the next mountain they wanted her to climb. There didn't seem to be any time or opportunity just to sit back after a successfully completed task, take a deep breath, and *enjoy* what had been accomplished.

As a result, Jennifer finally began to give up on trying to get her parents' approval or to achieve any real happiness through their approach. Instead, she began to rebel by putting less effort into her schoolwork and by dating boys she knew her parents disliked.

The home situation deteriorated to the point where Jennifer and her mom and dad rarely exchanged a civil word with one another. The parents also began to fear that she might elope with a boy who was a high school dropout. Predictably, the parents' reaction was to intensify their disapproval and be judgmental in their evaluations of her activities and choice of boyfriend.

Why had these parents begun to behave so as to provoke this crisis?

A major reason was that they had always been afraid of feeling too good about their own accomplishments. The mother's parents had treated her much as she was treating her own children. She had been taught that peak achievement was a worthy goal in itself, and anything less than the best was unacceptable.

The father's background had been somewhat different. He

had grown up in a poor family, where money was always a worry. Consequently, he had been conditioned to work diligently, succeed to his maximum capability, and prepare carefully for the future.

Although the sources of the attitudes of this mother and father differed, the end result added up to much the same approach to their eldest daughter: Jennifer was encouraged to work hard, expected to achieve significantly, and conditioned to believe that nothing she could accomplish would ever be enough. Consequently, she and her parents were unable to connect emotionally; they were blocked from establishing genuine lines of communication with one another.

In a common variation on this theme, ambitious parents who push their children toward the highest levels of performance may be driven by a desperate need to realize excessive, unrealistic expectations for their child. They somehow come to believe that their youngster is destined for greatness, and all other aspects of the parent-child relationship must be subordinated to this goal.

In general, these great expectations for our children are among the *major* roadblocks that prevent us from interacting enjoyably with them today. Instead of praising the present performances of our children, we tend to think, "Well, that was all right, but he didn't quite do what he should have done. There's still room for improvement."

One fourteen-year-old played a baseball game for his junior high school team at a level far above what he had accomplished in previous outings. In large part, the improvement in his performance was due to the fact that his father had worked with him in sessions outside his regular practices. The parent had taken the son to batting cages on weekends and drilled him strenuously on fielding techniques.

In past games, the boy had committed many errors and had not only gone hitless—he had completely failed to contact the ball with his bat. But in this game, he had played errorless ball, had been instrumental in two double-plays, and had grounded out once and flied out to left field twice.

His father's response? Instead of praising the youngster for his achievements—including the major accomplishment of at least making good contact with the ball while at the plate—Dad immediately began discussing once again what was wrong with the boy's batting. Needless to say, the conversation was quite deflating for the son, and it robbed the entire family of any joy they might have experienced.

After a series of such critiques, the son became so depressed that he told his parents he just couldn't take it anymore: "What's the point? I can't measure up, so why continue with this stuff?"

The boy in fact did quit the baseball team for the remainder of his junior high career. With the free time he now had available, he began to hang around with a group of kids who were into drugs. In a last-ditch effort to avert tragedy, a year of counseling finally enabled this family to begin to deal constructively with their problems.

I don't usually like to attach blame or point the finger. But the clear culprit in this case had been the father's expectations. In working on the ball field with his son, he had seen that the boy had great potential and that he was improving significantly with the extra practice. But instead of taking the progress step by step, he kept looking forward to some point in the future, when the teenager's performance might be perfect. In his fantasies, he saw the boy playing first-string on the high school team . . . then winning an athletic scholarship to college . . . and maybe even making the New York Yankees!

In most cases, hard work and practice help us all to improve

After a while, a child may tire of asking or wondering, "Have I performed well enough for you?"—which is just another way of asking, "Do you love me?" Instead, the teenager's conversation with you will focus on less threatening and more superficial issues.

For a true talking relationship to develop between a parent and teenager, then, the child must learn through the parent's example to love herself. Otherwise, like her mother and father, she will always be straining forward, but never able to celebrate or enjoy life fully. She'll never be free to appreciate the present moment, never free to engage in completely open, loving conversation.

The Emotionally Guarded Parent

Any parent who places a lid on emotional expression will automatically limit the possibilities of free and open communication with a teenager.

A number of parents, for example, believe that it's best to be on guard in relationships with others—and especially with teenagers. The reason? If you allow yourself or your loved ones to feel too good about anything, you'll have that much further to fall emotionally.

In contrast, by keeping your moods, including your feelings of happiness, at a lower, more even level, you'll be in a better position to protect your inner self. You'll have more emotional staying power and be less vulnerable to wide swings in your feelings.

Sometimes, this sort of wrongheaded, overly cautious "realism" may be expressed by a prevalent sense that the "ax is going to fall" because things are going too well in your life. Or one of the first thoughts that may come to mind is, "I know this is too good to last!"

Then again, the "realist" in you may cause you to push aside any intense, near-euphoric sense of well-being by whispering in your inner ear: "This is not reality. Don't forget that the *real* world isn't nearly this great."

Other parents may place an artificial ceiling on the excitement they'll let themselves or other family members experience. The parents of one twelve-year-old I encountered a number of years ago are a case in point.

The boy was a gifted athlete who often scored goals in soccer, hit home runs in baseball, and in general outperformed his peers on the playing fields. When he did well in one of these games, his first impulse, quite naturally, was to jump up and down and raise both his arms in a kind of victor's salute. Also, on the walk or drive home, he had a tendency to chatter with his friends and their parents about his achievements in the game.

When he was at an early age, this boy's parents—who were extremely concerned about not seeming conceited—cautioned him about talking too much about his achievements. "It's best to let others praise you, rather than praise yourself," his mother said.

When he won a trophy for winning several events in a track meet, his parents wouldn't even allow him to take it next door to show it to one of his best friends. "That can make people envious of you, and they may think you're just bragging," his father explained.

Time after time, his parents curbed and limited his enthusiasm until finally, it all but disappeared. He not only didn't share his triumphs with his peers and other "outsiders"; he didn't even feel free to talk to his parents about them.

When he became a teenager, this boy continued to perform well in sports. But by this point, he had developed a kind of stoic, reserved response when he did something well. For the most part, he was unable to express any excitement or even to enjoy his athletic activities fully—mainly because of the constraints his parents had placed upon him.

Even more worrisome, the boy became sexually involved with girls in his class, but he felt he had no adult to turn to to get advice about these relationships. His reluctance to talk about himself had spilled over to social and moral areas which demanded in-depth discussions and counseling—in which he was unable to engage.

The first challenge I faced when I began to work with this boy was to help him recapture some of the enthusiasm, wonder, and excitement he had originally experienced.

"Take a chance on being happy—and talk about the way you feel!" I told him. "If you do something great out there on the baseball field, you should be free to *feel* good about it, and to express those feelings."

As it turned out, this boy hadn't completely lost his ability to feel good about his accomplishments. He just hid those impulses. So as I encouraged him to tell me how great he felt, he responded rather readily. Before long, when he was congratulated by someone for his success, he began to feel free to acknowledge the accolades and even carry on conversations about how well he had done.

What was the response of those to whom he was "bragging"? In the first place, of course, it wasn't bragging at all. And the reaction of his friends and acquaintances was the exact opposite of what his parents had taught him to expect.

They had told him that people would envy him; that they would like him less; and that he would get a reputation as a "big head." In fact, though, he became a much more interesting person whom other people liked to be around.

Furthermore, learning to express his excitement at life was

the first step in talking about other feelings and concerns. Soon, he was revealing more freely his worries about his relationships with his various girlfriends. And with this greater openness came the possibility of healing of emotions and relationships.

In many respects, the willingness and ability to show emotion, and especially excitement, is one of the master keys to effective, compelling conversation—including conversations between parents and teenagers. Excited people are interesting people, while withholding people—those who place an artificial cap on their feelings—are crashing bores! So if you like what you do and are good at it and sometimes get excited about it, feel free to tell others! Most important of all, encourage your child to express her excitement.

The Saboteur

Think back on the last time that things seemed to be going particularly well in your life.

Perhaps you were feeling exceptionally happy and satisfied with your family or your career. Or maybe you made an especially meaningful contribution to your church or synagogue. Or you might have reached some milestone in your health, such as losing a lot of weight or reducing your cholesterol levels.

Then what happened, just after you began to feel so happy?

Perhaps an event intervened to make you feel *less* happy. If so, the chances are, *you* are the one who did something to help sabotage your own happiness, perhaps without even knowing what you were doing. Also, it's likely that as you reduced your happiness, you interfered with the happiness of those around you, including that of other family members.

Inevitably in these circumstances, the ability to talk—*really* talk—with one another will disappear. To avert this danger, you must become more alert to the ways that parents can sabotage their own happiness and their capacity to communicate with their teenagers. Here are a few typical "saboteurs" I've encountered:

- A father, who had been making progress in his relationship with his twelve-year-old son, had made a commitment to take the boy to school several days a week. The purpose of these times together was to give the father and son more opportunities to chat and enjoy one another.

   The plan worked quite well for a week or so. But then the father undercut the potential for happiness: Several nights in a row, he stayed up to watch the late movie on television. As a result, he was exhausted in the morning and became impatient and snappy with his son. Far from promoting a good relationship, their trips to school deteriorated to the point that the mother had to take over this responsibility.

- A mother had been trying to get her overweight sixteen-year-old daughter to lose some pounds, and finally, the girl went on a diet that seemed to be working. For the first time, she managed to stick to a low-calorie regimen for about a month. As part of her program, she completely eliminated the fatty fast-food hamburgers that she usually ate on weekends with her friends.

   But then, the daughter slipped: She raided the refrigerator one night and ate nearly a pint of ice cream. When the mother found out, she accused the girl mercilessly: "You'll never be disciplined enough to lose weight! Don't you care at all about your appearance? I'm ready to give up on you completely!"

   It's true that the mother had been under considerable pressure at work during the preceding week, and this lapse by her daughter pushed her completely over the edge. But regardless of the excuse, the outburst succeeded in making the girl feel worthless. As a result, she went off her diet completely. In effect, she tried to recapture a little of her lost happiness in food.

• A father always pushed advice and instruction too far —especially when things seemed particularly happy in the family. He'd correct his son or daughter once, but he wouldn't stop there. Instead, he'd go on and on:

"You understand what I'm getting at, don't you? If you keep acting that way, there's no telling where it might lead. Let me give you an example . . ."

Before long, the exasperated child would react angrily, and whatever peace and joy the family was experiencing would evaporate—simply because the father had become a saboteur of the household's happiness.

One of the best ways I've discovered to avoid this kind of sabotage and also enhance genuine talking relationships with teenagers is to eliminate what I call the "benephobic language" from your vocabulary. This means getting rid of the qualifiers, conditional phrases, and criticisms in family conversations.

For starters, try this exercise:

Step 1   List all the "benephobic language" that you typically use. These are words, phrases, and "principles to live by" that help place a cap on your ability to let yourself go and celebrate unreservedly in life. I'm talking about such cautionary, downbeat responses as these:

• "Don't get a big head about your success."
• "God will take your blessings away if you focus on them too much."

- "The ax is going to fall."
- "Every good thing must come to an end."
- "Everyone will disappoint you at some point."
- "That's a good job, *but* . . ."

It may take a day or two to get most of your recurrent be-nephobic language down on paper, but keep at it until you have a fairly complete list.

Step 2   For one day, try avoiding the use of this benephobic language completely, even when you think it's more "honest" or "helpful" or "forthright" to throw in some of those qualifiers and conditioners.

Step 3   Try avoiding your typical benephobic language for one more day.

Step 4   On the third day, continue to avoid the benephobic talk, but also resolve to say only positive things about other people. Up to this point, you've tried to eliminate the set, recurrent qualifiers you often use. Now you're ready to tackle the totality of your responses to other people and to daily situations.

In short, don't criticize *at all*—and that includes even "constructive criticism." Don't inject negative observations *at all*.

Finally, when a negative thought comes into your mind, try to replace it immediately with a positive thought. (For example, "That woman certainly is poorly dressed—but on the other hand, she may be a person who focuses more on deeper values than on outward appearance. It would be interesting to meet her and find out what she's really like.")

You may feel that much, a little, or none of the foregoing descriptions of different types of parents applies to you. But that's not important. The fundamental thing to understand is that you must learn to enjoy your teenager before you can really talk to him or her. And the chances are, whatever blocks there are in your ability to communicate with that boy or girl begin with *you*, not with your child.

Once you've begun to deal with your own parental obstacles to an open relationship, you shouldn't continue to focus exclusively on yourself and on any problems you may face. Rather, it's also necessary to understand what motivates, interests, and bothers your child. So now, let's take a closer look at the teenager in your family.

CHAPTER 3

What Kind of Kid Do You Have?

Your teenager may seem closed off, secretive, and generally uncommunicative at home, and that can be quite disturbing and disappointing to a parent—especially if the change in behavior has come rather abruptly.

Only a year or so ago, when his elementary school experience was in full flower, he may have been quite open and talkative. In those days, perhaps he showed his love and attachment to you freely. You seemed to be the center of his life, as he was of yours.

But now, things are different. Why the drastic change?

There are probably a number of forces at work. In the first place, as a typical contemporary adolescent, he's most likely so preoccupied with the present pressures and future uncertainties of his life that he just doesn't have the energy or inclination to reach out to parents or siblings.

Also, a major characteristic of a child's development at this stage of life is the drive for independence. He may in fact love and respect you, but he needs to "spread his wings." Also, he may suspect that now he knows more than you do in some areas, and consequently, he wants the opportunity to solve various problems on his own.

But he's finding this new independence is not so easy. So when the teenage years arrive, a child's anxieties have often multiplied out of control. You feel for him because it's apparent to you that your child feels weighed down by competitive challenges, social pressures, and real or imagined failures. Yet, he won't open up and tell you what he's feeling so that you can sympathize and provide help.

A typical teenage response when a parent tries to enter into a conversation on the deeper levels—a response which may begin as early as age nine or ten—often goes something like this: "I don't want to talk about it." Or, "I'd rather not get into that now." Or, "Later, Mom, I've got things to do."

So how do you break through to your teenager under these circumstances?

If you've worked with as many children as I have—or for that matter, after you've made an effort over the years just to draw out the children in your own family—your approach in conversation will become intuitive. You'll simply know in your heart or your "guts," in those inner faculties that transcend any logic or self-help technique, how to engage in intimate talk with your teenager.

But most times, before intuition can take over, it's necessary first to *learn* how to find and use those basic principles that control parent-child relationships and communication.

Certainly, in my own case, intuition didn't appear full-blown as a seasoned ability to draw others out in conversation. Like most other people, I had to learn how to understand and approach others. But fortunately, in my interactions with my mother and father, I began to learn some of these important principles at a very early age. As a result, they've become almost as natural and intuitive for me as breathing.

As a first step in developing this sort of intuition, I'd suggest that you take a few days, beginning right now, to observe your teenager. Watch the way he reacts at the dinner table or in other family gatherings. When does he laugh? When does she seem bored? What makes her withdraw?

As you watch your child respond, you'll automatically be observing the rest of the family and home environment. You may notice that your husband ignores your child's effort to reach out for help. Or you may observe that seemingly innocent comments by your wife—such as reminders about personal appearance or grades—"set off" your daughter, provoking her to run off to her room in a rage.

As you proceed with this exercise, it will be helpful to take notes on what you see. Don't be afraid to jot down some tentative conclusions about how certain dynamics in the family are exacerbating relationships. During this process, you'll begin to get a better picture about what makes your teenager "tick." Most important of all, you'll start to understand those dominant traits that may be making his or her life miserable—and impeding real parent-child talk.

Next, after this period of initial observation, you'll be ready to answer the questions in the following Kid Type Questionnaire. There are no right or wrong answers in this exercise. Rather, the questions have been designed to help you determine some of the most important characteristics of your teenager. Then, with this understanding you'll be in a better position to identify his Kid Type (or Kid Types, if he has more than one set of dominant traits).

So now, move ahead and respond as well as you can with a "true" or a "false" to each of the statements in the following

ten numbered groups. Even though you may not be entirely comfortable with a simple true or false, give the answer that comes
closest to describing how you feel. Then, I'll help you interpret
your responses after you've finished.

Note: Each set of statements is intended to apply to children
of either sex, except the statements introduced by the phrase "For
parents of boys."

THE KID TYPE QUESTIONNAIRE

Group 1

- My teenager seems to have a deep need always to have
  a steady dating relationship with a member of the opposite sex.
- I suspect that my child is sexually promiscuous.
- My child seems to be an active homosexual.
- Much of the time, my teenager appears to have members
  of the opposite sex on the mind.
- My child is constantly on the phone with a member of
  the opposite sex.

Group 2 For Parents of Boys

- Girls are always calling my son or asking him to go
  places with them.
- My son seems almost lackadaisical about his girlfriends,
  but for some reason, they fall all over themselves to
  compete for his attention.
- My son typically leaves it up to his date to decide what
  they'll do or where they'll go on an outing.
- The mother in our family makes most of the domestic
  decisions, including decisions about the son's activities
  and future.

Group 3

- My teenager periodically has angry outbursts.
- Since reaching adolescence, my child has physically attacked a parent.
- I'm afraid of my teenager.
- I sense that my child is frequently angry or hostile toward various situations or people.
- My child is quick to laugh at others or make fun of them.
- My teenager seems to have more negative than positive things to say about other people or situations.
- My child often holds grudges against other people, including family members or individuals outside the family.
- My child has on occasion threatened me with some sort of retaliation when I have failed to bend to his will.
- Sometimes, my teenager just seems to have a mean streak.

Group 4

- My child has left home without warning for at least a twenty-four-hour period.
- My teenager has run away from home at least once.
- My child hangs out with kids who have left home or town for unannounced excursions lasting two days or longer.

Group 5

- My teenager always insists on wearing the wildest, craziest clothes.
- He likes to buy trendy-looking clothes or accessories typically worn by rock groups or other popular entertainers.

- My child insists on wearing outlandish hairdos—even when I object.
- Although I may feel that certain styles are inappropriate for one's sex—such as earrings for a man—my teenager wants to experiment with those styles anyway.

Group 6

- My teenager always has to have his (or her) own way.
- My child will often try to play one parent off against another.
- Even when I put my foot down on some issue, I can expect my teenager to do as he likes—and then perhaps say my directions weren't clear.
- Since he was quite small, my child has been rather wild, in that he's prone to break or damage other people's property, get into scraps with other children, or "talk back" to adults.
- My teenager likes to take risks.
- My child favors relatively dangerous activities, such as high-speed bicycle races, skateboard acrobatics, or riding in fast cars.
- I find that my child is quite difficult to control.

Group 7

- My child frequently seems bored.
- My teenager often complains about "not having anything to do."
- When some activity is suggested, a typical response from my teenager may go like this: "That doesn't sound like any fun." Or "I'm too tired." Or "I just don't feel like that right now."

Group 8

- My child is extremely reluctant to share her feelings with me.
- My child seems quite secretive.
- My teenager frequently locks the door to his room or otherwise forbids admittance.
- I suspect that my child is involved with drugs, marijuana, or alcohol.
- My teenager hangs out with kids who I suspect use drugs, marijuana, or alcohol.
- When I try to engage my child in a discussion about drugs, marijuana, or alcohol, he either refuses to talk about it or avoids the subject.
- My child seems to have trouble showing excitement or otherwise expressing emotion.
- There frequently seems to be a lack of connection between my child's feelings and the things she chooses to talk about (e.g., I may sense that something, such as a difficult relationship at school, is bothering her deeply, but she may refuse to discuss this problem or pretend it doesn't exist).

Group 9

- My child is overly sensitive about wrongs he perceives he may have done.
- My teenager has a great capacity for feeling guilt.
- After my child has done something wrong and I correct him, he'll still check to be sure I accept and love him (e.g., he may ask several times, "Do you really forgive me?" or "Are you sure it's all right?").

- My child seems to have an uncontrollable inner need to get involved in entirely too many activities.
- My teenager is a perfectionist—even one mistake on a test may cause her great anxiety or trigger a depression.
- My child is extremely competitive, with a deep need to win or be the best—and when he loses or does worse than he hoped, he gets very upset.

Group 10

- My child has often become a victim or target of derision or abuse by his peers at school, in extracurricular activities, or in other social situations.
- My teenager seems reluctant to assert herself in situations where I feel she should be assertive.
- My child is always a follower, never a leader.
- When another child tells my teenager to do something, he'll usually obey.
- I know or suspect that my child has been the victim of sexual or other abuse by an adult.
- I've noticed bruises, cuts, or other signs of violence on my child's body.
- Much of the time, my child seems rather unhappy or morose.
- Many times, my teenager appears to be frightened or unusually wary in the presence of a particular adult.

Now, with your answers in front of you, let's turn to the interpretation of this questionnaire.

INTERPRETING THE KID TYPE QUESTIONNAIRE

In watching and evaluating the children under my care during the past two decades, I've identified a number of "Kid Types," or groupings of key personal traits that may signal problem areas and verbal roadblocks to open communication.

Each of the numbered groupings in the above questionnaire corresponds to a particular Kid Type, which I'll be describing for you shortly. If you know your teenager's special characteristics, as reflected by these Kid Types, you'll be in a much stronger position to break through to the deeper levels of intimacy which you're missing now as a parent.

Of course, I know that no list of Kid Types can be exhaustive or neatly cover all the traits of every child. Furthermore, you shouldn't assume that any child must fit neatly into only one of these categories. In fact, your teenager may display the characteristics of several of these Kid Types. Still, most parents with "talking problems" should find at least some of the important traits of their teenager lurking in one or more of these descriptions.

At this point in the book, I'll only provide a brief sketch of each of the Kid Types as a means to move you closer to a talking relationship with your child. Later, as we explore the various Types in greater detail, you'll likely see more situations and characteristics that you can identify with in your family. The main purpose of this exercise is just to encourage you to think more deeply about *your* teenager and to help you take the first step in establishing a real talking relationship with him.

Now, here is a list of ten common Kid Types I've identified over the years—and an explanation of how they are related to the questionnaire you've just answered. Again, you'll note that in each case the number of the Kid Type corresponds to the numbered group of statements in the questionnaire.

Kid Type #1

If you answered "true" to any of the statements in Group 1 on the questionnaire, your child may be a *Relationship Addict*.

This child, often a girl, lives for sexual relationships. In most cases, the encounters involve those with the opposite sex, though sometimes homosexuality becomes a factor. The main need is not for the sex but for the acceptance and warmth that such an intimate connection seems able to offer.

The parents' challenge: determining the underlying family cause of the addiction and then finding ways to adjust the family interactions accordingly.

Kid Type #2

If you answered "true" to any of the statements in Group 2 on the questionnaire, your child may be a *Weak Romeo*.

Usually a boy, this teenager expects members of the opposite sex to seek him out and then seduce him. Predominantly a passive personality, he willingly becomes promiscuous but rarely takes the initiative. In general, he's unable to enter into genuine, open communication because he really doesn't know how to talk to girls on an open, mature level.

The parents' challenge: identifying precisely the lack of communication between the child and one or both parents. Then, communication skills and a mature form of intimacy with both parents and outsiders can be taught more effectively to the youngster.

Kid Type #3

If you answered "true" to any of the statements in Group 3 on the questionnaire, your child may be an *Angry Child*.

This child can't control his temper or has failed to learn appropriate ways to express anger. There are several possibilities: Like a volcano poised to erupt, he may need only a slight, seemingly innocuous provocation to spew abuse out on dismayed parents. Or he may stifle his angry feelings, only to see them emerge as depression or some other emotional problem.

In some cases, the teenager's hostility may even be expressed in physically violent parent abuse. Others may direct their anger toward outsiders, such as through drug abuse or vandalism.

The parents' challenge: to find the source of the child's anger, open up lines of communication which will enable him to talk about his problem, and then help the youngster design an action plan to resolve his anger.

Kid Type #4

If you answered "true" to any of the statements in Group 4 on the questionnaire, your child may be a *Runaway*.

Generally, I distinguish between two types of runaways—the young adolescents who are at the highest risk from dangerous situations or unscrupulous adults, and the older teenagers who are better able to take care of themselves. The younger children must be controlled more strictly, while the older ones generally have to be given more rope.

The parents' challenge: finding a balance between giving the teenager adequate freedom of movement—thus showing him that he's trusted—and at the same time protecting him from his own indiscretions and poor judgment.

Kid Type #5

If you answered "true" to any of the statements in Group 5 on the questionnaire, your child may be a *Weird Dresser*.

Parents often major in minors as they focus on their teenager's bizarre choices of clothing and yet overlook more serious, festering problems in the relationship. Far from being a major threat to parental authority, weird dressing by an adolescent can be a way to embark on some more open and creative communication. At the same time, the parent who can succeed in getting through to the Weird Dresser may be able to head off image problems the child may not be mature enough to anticipate.

The parents' challenge: keeping a sense of perspective *and* a sense of humor about the child's sartorial selections.

Kid Type #6

If you answered "true" to any of the statements in Group 6 on the questionnaire, your child may be a *Wild Child*.

This youngster may seem completely unpredictable and out of control. He may also be accident-prone, a chronic risk-taker, or a mischief-maker and miscreant.

Some variations of the Wild Child can be as adept at identifying strengths and weaknesses in parents and family relationships as Machiavelli was at understanding the manipulation of political power. She can play one parent off against the other or otherwise orchestrate personality interactions at home to achieve personal ends.

The parents' challenge: to direct the exuberance, creativity, independence, and initiative of this child into more productive pursuits.

Kid Type #7

If you answered "true" to any of the statements in Group 7 on the questionnaire, your child may be a *Bored Child*.

There are a number of reasons that children may become bored. These include a deep-rooted anger that is expressed as boredom; an overload of activities that has drained the child of energy; or simply the child's failure to become involved in an activity that really interests him—a problem that can often be corrected by sound, sensitive parental guidance.

The parents' challenge: to get to the bottom of the boredom through in-depth discussions with the child and then to help her plan ways to introduce more interest and excitement into her life.

Kid Type #8

If you answered "true" to any of the statements in Group 8 on the questionnaire, your child may be a *Clam*.

The Clam is typically secretive, avoids interaction with parents, or otherwise seeks isolation from family members, or peers, or both. Of course, some children are naturally "loners," and there is nothing inherently wrong with that. In addition, a child may be secretive merely because he's growing up and wants his privacy. Refusing to share something with a parent may just be a way of expressing the natural process of separation and independence.

But excessive isolation from parents or classmates can also reflect significant emotional problems and may impede the teenager's ability to reach his full personal potential. For example, a growing tendency toward secretiveness may mask serious problems like drug use, unwise sexual involvement, or dangerous criminal activity.

The parents' challenge: to evaluate the extent to which the child's individual emotional makeup is causing him to spend so much time alone or to avoid normal communication with parents or friends. Then, the parent must find ways to guide the teenager toward some degree of healthy involvement with other people— while at the same time respecting the need for privacy.

Kid Type #9

If you answered "true" to any of the statements in Group 9 on the questionnaire, your child may be an *Insecure Child*.

Some insecure children are characterized by excessive feelings of guilt; they seem to assume that most of the time, others are right and they are wrong or to blame. These youngsters may feel remorseful or become apologetic when others challenge them—even though they may have been entirely correct in their attitudes or actions.

The other side of coin is the insecure overachiever who on the outside, at least, appears to be completely in control. These teenagers work hard to reach beyond themselves and their natural capacities, many times because they are trying to compensate for deep inner feelings that they somehow fall short.

A number of these overachievers will play a major role in shaping the future of our society. But this group also includes many children who become exceedingly unhappy when they fail to achieve their objectives; as a result, they may develop serious emotional problems.

The parents' challenge: to break through to a deeper level of communication and help the Insecure Child understand that she is accepted unconditionally by Mom and Dad, regardless of what she does or fails to do.

Kid Type #10

If you answered "true" to any of the statements in Group 10 on the questionnaire, your child may be a *Victim*.

Many teenagers have been victims of sexual or other abuse at the hands of a parent, uncle or aunt, teacher, or other adult. The child's ability to talk about this problem to a "safe" adult is an absolutely essential first step toward stopping the abuse and then beginning the process of emotional healing.

The parents' challenge: overcoming adult denial or ignorance of the existence of the abuse, and then taking immediate steps to remove the child from the risk or danger. More effective counseling can then begin.

In less severe circumstances, the child may have become a kind of doormat for bullies or others who sense that he won't retaliate to their aggression.

These children may also be nice kids who give in to the demands of more aggressive youngsters. They may not compromise basic moral values when under pressure, but still they need to be encouraged to assert themselves more and to use the power at their disposal.

The parents' challenge: getting timid children to stand up for themselves, both in the family and among outsiders.

You may already recognize your child among these brief descriptions, but if not, don't become concerned. The main idea right now is just to recognize the main traits and characteristics of the child who is living with you. Once you've done that, you'll be in a stronger position to understand that teenager and establish a more meaningful parent-child relationship.

As I indicated previously in introducing this list, we'll be exploring each of these Kid Types in some detail in later chapters in this book. First, however, let's turn to one more set of basic skills for those who want to learn to talk with a teenager—what I call the Seven Secrets of Successful Communication with your children.

CHAPTER 4

The Seven Secrets of Successful Communication

Art Linkletter once said that starting up a conversation with a difficult person is somewhat like devising a strategy to score a touchdown against a tough football team. The main objective is to break through the other person's defenses, force him to respond to you on his own turf, and finally "score a goal" by encouraging him to engage in an intimate, thought-provoking discussion with you.

In many ways, teenagers these days often qualify as "difficult" people with multiple defenses and a seeming lack of interest in heart-to-heart talks with parents. But with well-formulated strategies, these children *can* be encouraged to open up and relate on deeper levels with their mothers and fathers.

What are the best strategies to achieve these ends? I've summed up my favorites in the form of "Seven Secrets of Successful Communication." These are the basic approaches that will crop up again and again in our discussion of different Kid Types.

WHAT ARE THE SEVEN SECRETS—AND HOW CAN I USE THEM?

Secret #1: Each Family Member Has a Job Description

Every family member has certain tasks he should perform and goals he should strive to fulfill. To function effectively, parents must understand the details of their "job description" and also that of their children's.

The crux of the parent's job is to set limits and rules of behavior in the family. The child's job, on the other hand, is to test and struggle against those rules. It's during the process of this struggle that the rules become clear and firm and that the child comes to understand them and make them his own in preparation for adulthood.

The parent, for instance, must establish certain moral values that both children and parents are expected to obey. The parent may say, "It's important to be honest" or, "You shouldn't steal" or, "Treat others as you would like to have them treat you."

The child, for his part, must act as the "moral security agent" in the sense that he becomes the person who tests those rules. He needs to see if the parent has really been serious in establishing and following certain standards of conduct. Also, it's important for him to become convinced that the parents' rules can stand up to the hard knocks that are delivered in the real world.

To this end, the child may at some point lie, cheat, or steal. In some way, he'll push and tear away at the rules and principles laid down by the parents. Also, he may periodically try to catch the parent in some value-related inconsistency and then accuse, "You said that was wrong—why are you doing it?"

For example, a child may pressure his parent to allow him to drive or drink before the legal age, and the parent may assume that this bending of the rules is a way to ingratiate himself to the child. But later, the child may turn around and bring up this very same leniency, which at the time seemed to be solely for the child's benefit, as a criticism of the parent!

My son Scott and I went on a holiday together several years ago to an amusement park where my own father and I used to go when I was a kid. But when we arrived at the park, we found that it had been closed to the public that day so that some special group could use the facilities. Scott was obviously disappointed, and so was I. So I decided to try to lie to those in charge in an effort to convince them that we were entitled to enter the premises with the special group. My argument worked, and before long, we were inside, all ready to enjoy the place.

But then Scott dropped a bomb: "Say, is it OK for me to do what you did to get in here if there's something I want that much?"

I stopped, looked at him for a moment and replied, "No, it's not OK. Let's get out of here—fast!"

Although it probably wasn't entirely conscious, Scott was just doing his job as my son, testing me and the values that I had taught him. I've known other kids who convinced parents to write notes saying they were sick, when they really weren't sick. Then, the children would be the first to point up the parents' inconsistency.

A child's successful development depends in part on how well these tensions between the parent's job and the child's job are resolved. When the parent projects an image of consistency between what he says and what he does—despite the pressure the child puts on the parent to live up to his stated principles—the child will have a good role model for the development of solid values.

Secret #2: Successful Parents Know How to Play Family Games

Certainly, rearing a teenager is serious business, but the experience should also be fun and interesting!

To emphasize the pleasurable side of parenting, I like to think of many parent-child interactions in terms of games. Sometimes there are winners and sometimes there are losers in these family contests, but the play should always be something of a frolic. Both parent and child should leave these encounters with feelings of satisfaction and accomplishment.

I've found over the years that most successful and productive parent-teen talking relationships can be summed up in terms of two common childhood games—red rover and pick-up-sticks.

Red Rover   As you'll probably recall from your elementary school days, red rover is a game that is frequently played like this:

The children divide up into two equal teams, and then the two teams retreat to opposite sides of the yard or playground. Next, each team joins hands and faces the other team. One team proceeds to chant in unison, "Red rover, red rover, send [the name of a child on the opposing team] right over!"

The child who has been named must then race across the yard to the team that has called him and try to break through the line they've formed. If he does break through, he gets to return to his team with one of the children on the opposing team in tow. On the other hand, if he fails to break through, he has to join his opponents' line.

The other team then takes its turn in chanting out "red rover, red rover" and tries to hold off the opposing player it has called over.

The teams continue to alternate the "red rover" chant until

one of the teams is left with only one player, or the game is stopped for some other reason. The team which has the most players at the end of the game is the winner.

So what does this have to do with talking to your teenager?

The lesson for parents of adolescents is that you should *expect* your child to try to break through the "lines" of values or behavior standards that you've set up. At the same time, though, those lines or limits must be established on safe ground.

You wouldn't set up a red-rover line on the edge of a cliff, for instance, where a child might plunge to destruction. Similarly, you also should lay down the limits of behavior and conduct in your family in areas where the child can "break through," either by rebelling or making a mistake, and still not be placed seriously at risk.

For example, I always encourage parents to draw hard, firm lines with such things as caffeine consumption, wearing crazy clothing, or cigarette use. Then, be ready to fight tooth and nail to maintain those standards, or at least negotiate very stringently in establishing amendments to the standards.

One set of parents came to me with a deep concern that their fifteen-year-old girl was going to get involved in the drug culture that was rampant at the suburban high school she was about to enter. The school was known for cocaine and alcohol abuse, and her classmates were already talking about looking forward to going to parties where these substances were in use.

My advice went something like this:

• First of all, set rather strict guidelines for drinks containing caffeine, and also for a curfew. (These suggestions arose directly out of this particular family situation: The parents, as it happened, felt their daughter was consuming too many colas and other beverages containing caffeine. Also, they had been feeling the pressure from her to allow her to stay out later at night on weekends.)

• Second, fight hard to maintain these rules, but don't be completely rigid. Let your daughter win sometimes. (In this case, they did allow her to drink a certain number of cola beverages on weekends and also gave in and let her stay out an extra hour on occasion.)

• Third, expect that by focusing your attention mainly on these "safe" issues, you'll have less worry about the really *big* issues, like drugs or dangerous sex.

Sure enough, in this case, arguments between the parents and their daughter centered entirely on their battles over caffeine and the curfew. Consequently, the girl was spared having to deal with more threatening issues.

In other words, if you lose a little on strange clothes, caffeine, an occasional late date, or even an occasional cigarette, you haven't lost much. On the other hand, if you're easy on these issues and the main fights occur over drugs or sexual promiscuity, then you're battling on the edge of a real cliff. If your child "breaks through the Red Rover line" here, disaster could be the result. Parents must be willing to draw the lines of battle well before their child faces true danger.

Pick-Up-Sticks Another important family game is similar to pick-up-sticks. In the real childhood game, the sticks are dropped randomly, and it's nobody's fault how they land. The only question is how the player with the turn is going to pick up each of the sticks, one by one in an orderly fashion, without disturbing the other sticks.

The analogy to parent-teen interactions goes like this:

You're often presented with a difficult situation or condition that nobody really created or can alter. In such a case, you have to learn to tackle the challenge or problem in your teen's life or in your relationship *without trying to attach blame* or point the finger. If teenager *or* parent is at fault, that fact will quickly become evident without anyone have to belabor the issue.

For example, many families I've encountered find that big arguments or crises often occur when one or more of the family members are excessively tired. After one argument that occurred between a teenage boy and his mother and father at the end of a particularly trying day, the boy left home for several hours and resorted to alcohol and drug use. He had given up these activities a month before, but felt he needed to let off steam and "feel good" after the argument.

What precipitated the argument? There was no particular issue, just mutual attacks of fatigue and frustration. The father had experienced a long, bad day at the office; and the mother had become exasperated after arguments with another child in the family. As for the boy, he was tired and hungry and had been especially frustrated that day with his inability to improve his grades.

When the teenager had arrived home looking for comfort and help with his efforts to be a better student, he had been confronted instead with criticism and testiness from his parents. So he had decided, "What's the use?" and had headed out for a meeting with his drug- and alcohol-using friends.

In this case, instead of "pick-up-sticks," the parents had played a game that might better be called "kick and destroy the sticks!" Rather than dealing coolly, patiently, and individually with the boy's genuine concerns about his schoolwork, they had unloaded all their frustrations on him. He had received the blame not only for the shape of his life, but also for the shambles the parents were experiencing in their own. In effect, he was the main one being charged with the way the "sticks" in the family had fallen!

That's no way to play pick-up-sticks, and it's also no way to deal with a teenager's concerns and difficulties. If you just approach your teenager's problems nonjudgmentally, as you would a game, you'll find yourself making much more progress, and perhaps even enjoying the challenge.

Secret #3: Parents Must Become Experts at the Power Play

Obviously, most if not all of the real power in the family resides in the parents, especially when the children are young. But as a child moves into the teen years, the power centers begin to shift so that more power becomes available to the child.

At this stage of development, it's important for children to realize that they *do* have increasing amounts of power, and also that they must learn to use that power wisely. Furthermore, it's the job of the parent to *empower* the youngster—or allow him to become more independent and responsible in his world.

On the other hand, the parent who is merely an enabler may find the child always looks back over the shoulder, hoping for parental support or direction. Those who enable typically provide ready props and supports, along with a safety net to prevent painful falls and failures. Those who focus on empowering will give lessons and instructions, but then they'll take a hands-off attitude, as the child tries to operate on his own.

During the teen years the child must be encouraged to "fly solo" in an increasing number of ways, even if he doesn't always execute perfect takeoffs, landings, and other key maneuvers in his relationships. One sixteen-year-old boy, Arnie, was having trouble telling a pushy woman, the owner of a local clothing store, that he didn't want to work for her. She was the mother of one of his classmates, and when she had heard that he was looking for a part-time job, she immediately starting putting pressure on him to take a sales position in her shop.

But Arnie was reluctant. For one thing, her motives were unclear. She was divorced; he was big for his age and rather handsome; and she was known as a flirt. Did she have sexual designs on the boy? He didn't know, and he didn't want to find out. Also, he wasn't sure he wanted a sales position that would require him to work the weekend hours that she needed.

Unfortunately, however, the older woman wouldn't back off and let Arnie make up his mind in peace. Instead, she called him up several times to press her case. Also, she "accidentally" ran into him on a couple of occasions in the shopping mall where her store was located and where he sometimes got ice cream with his friends.

Arnie's parents learned about the situation as a result of a word or two their son dropped: "I'm looking for a job, and I've got an offer, but I don't know about this store owner. She seems a little pushy."

Little by little, in the context of a relaxed family discussion, Arnie revealed some of his concerns about the woman's motives. The parents just listened at this point without much comment, except for the father's suggestion to "take your time and check the whole situation out. There's no pressure on you."

When Arnie had left the room, his mother wanted to get on the phone and tell the older woman to look elsewhere. But the father wisely counseled her to "lay off and let him handle it. He's got to learn how to resolve these things on his own."

So the parents eased into the role of advisers to their son. When he saw they were treating him as a mature person and were going to let him make his own decision, he opened up to them even more, and together, they formulated a plan to deal with the situation.

In brief, Arnie decided not to take the job, but he also knew that to "get this woman off my back" he would have to tell her directly about his decision. So the next time he was at the mall, he walked right into her shop, pulled her aside, and told her he couldn't take the job because it wasn't quite what he was looking for.

To his increasing frustration, she kept on pressing him, until finally he said in an annoyed tone, "Look, I appreciate the offer, but I really don't want this job, OK?"

The woman was clearly taken aback and then she seemed to get a little angry herself. But Arnie didn't wait for any further response. He just walked out.

As Arnie recounted the incident to his parents, they were initially jarred by the rough way he had handled the woman. His father said, "Maybe you should have been a little easier on her. You can usually get the point across without making the other person mad."

But this time, it was the mother who understood better how the learning process was occurring with their son: "I think Arnie did just fine," she said. "Sure, it's easy to say after the fact that he should have done this or that, but we weren't there, and he was! Besides, this woman seemed a little thick-headed to me. I think he probably got the point across the only way he could!"

The father quickly agreed, and Arnie felt vindicated. Even more important, he had learned how to assert himself forcefully and exercise his power effectively outside the family.

To be sure, as he gains experience in this sort of thing, he can be expected to operate more smoothly. But it's in the nature of the learning process to learn as you go along and gain experience. For a first outing in using this sort of power, he had done rather well—and his parents had reinforced the lesson so that he would be encouraged to try again.

Secret #4: Courage Is the Key to Parent-Child Combat

Every family with teenagers can expect significant levels of verbal combat. Far from being primarily destructive, however, this conflict can become an extremely important training ground for children to learn how to handle arguments reasonably and maturely.

But in engaging in verbal combat, parents must have courage. They must learn not to avoid or deny the existence of conflict. Many times, when a parent denies that disagreement exists, or reacts passively to a challenge from a teenager, the child will escalate his aggression in an effort to get a response. Then, if there's still an inadequate parental reaction, the child will escalate again and perhaps again—frequently with destructive results.

One fourteen-year-old stepchild, Larry, harbored significant anger toward his stepfather. But the stepfather, feeling self-conscious and even a little guilty that he had taken over the position of the boy's real father, refused to stand up to the boy's expressions of anger.

At first, the anger came out as arguments initiated by Larry. Then, the boy began to use verbal abuse and profanity against the stepfather. Finally, he resorted to physical attacks, sometimes punching, kicking, or throwing objects at the adult. The boy's mother protested at this parent abuse, but she had always assumed it was the man's job to handle such rebellion, and so she kept her distance from the confrontations.

Eventually, Larry got involved in fighting people outside the family, in drug abuse, and in sexual promiscuity. When the parents finally realized they had totally lost control, they enrolled Larry in a school for teenagers with behavior problems.

Throughout the interchanges between this parent and child, Larry was looking for an appropriate response from one of the most important authority figures in his life, his stepfather. Failing to get such a reaction, he did all he knew to do: He tried again and again, escalating his actions in increasingly obnoxious and destructive ways.

During family therapy which occurred both when Larry was at school and at home on vacations, the stepfather finally realized that he had to meet the boy's anger head-on. In short, he had to display a little courage in his dealings with his son.

The basic technique he used was a disarmingly simple one that I've advocated for years, what I call "Uncle Mikey's stop-it therapy."

Most parents make things far too complicated in their dealings with their children. They forget the tremendous power of an authoritative, unequivocal, no-nonsense command from a parent, and especially a father. One of the best of these commands is just to say sternly, without qualification or waffling, "Stop it!"

Usually, you don't even have to state what the consequences will be if the child fails to stop whatever he's doing. The implied, "If you don't stop it, I'll do something that will really make you sorry" is frequently all that's required.

That was the approach Larry's stepfather used. Larry started yelling at his mother about some inconsequential issue, and the stepfather suddenly stepped in, eyeball-to-eyeball, and growled, "Stop it!"

Larry *did* stop—immediately. Total shock registered on his face. Then, pulling himself together, he did what all children will do: He tested the new limits that were being imposed. He gave his stepfather a push, a response that would have gone unanswered in the past. But this time, the adult, who was considerably bigger and heavier than Larry, roughly shoved the boy's arms away. At the same time, he responded in an even louder tone, "I said *stop it!*"

Larry really didn't know what to make of this new turn of

events. Here was a limit on his conduct that he couldn't push through, physically or otherwise. If he tried another shove, he might get pushed back on his can, or worse! So he reverted to verbal abuse—which once again, the stepfather met with a "Stop it, Larry! Right now!"

And Larry did stop it. Continuing to swear under his breath but obviously subdued, he marched off to his room, and the confrontation was over. Now, with the stepfather taking a more authoritative role, the focus of Larry's life became a bit clearer.

Of course, much more needed to be done in the healing of this relationship. Larry and his stepfather began to have a series of conversations about what would be expected of him as a member of the family—and what his privileges would be if he observed the rules. If he violated the rules, the consequences were also clear: Larry stood to lose privileges, such as money for movies or other outings.

There were plenty of arguments and confrontations, but now, the level of conflict had become manageable. Also, the further this stepfather and stepson moved along in their relationship, the more the boy entered into the negotiations for the rules. Larry was encouraged to participate because his stepfather was reasonable in providing additional privileges in return for good conduct.

So this parent, who had allowed his son to go out of control, was able to act effectively after finding a reservoir of personal courage. He had feared a violent reaction the first time he tried to stand up to the boy, and that's certainly what he got. But after standing up to that initial onslaught, he was able to lay down standards of conduct that changed not only his life, but that of his stepson.

As for Larry, he soon got used to the new regime his stepfather had established. Furthermore, although he would never have admitted it, the system clearly gave him some security he had lacked before. Now, he had the limits he had been seeking so desperately.

Secret #5: Learn to Avoid the Sieve Syndrome

Let's return for a moment to an aspect of that fear of happiness that I've called "benephobia." You'll recall that one of the main things that stands in the way of a good talking relationship between parents and teenagers is a failure to enjoy one another. And one of the main obstacles to enjoying another person is an inability to love, accept, and enjoy yourself.

Yet, for a productive parent-child relationship to develop, it's essential for *both* the adult *and* the teen to feel good about themselves. They must each be able to forgive themselves; receive forgiveness; accept their own strengths (as well as weaknesses); and celebrate their personal triumphs and successes.

In my opinion, those who are unable to feel good about themselves are like *sieves*: They are never able to be filled up with compliments or a sense of satisfaction about their achievements. Instead, there are "holes" in their personalities through which the goodness escapes, only to leave a sense of emptiness or lost well-being.

One fifteen-year-old boy, Tom, was always looking for compliments, but nothing I could ever say would satisfy him. A typical exchange:

> Tom: "Am I doing my job any better?"
> Me: "Yes."
> Tom: "Better than I used to?"
> Me: "Yes."
> Tom: "Better than last month?"

I never let this sort of dialogue go any further. I'd always call Tom on his constant pleading for compliments or stroking.

"You're being needy," I told him on more than one occasion. "You're behaving like a sieve. Everything nice I say to you goes right through you. There's nothing I can do to make you take in what I say. But if you're going to feel good about yourself, you *must* take it in. It's your choice. So let's stop playing this game."

Finally, it began to register on Tom what he was doing. He gradually stopped pleading with me and others and for extra compliments and actually started taking compliments at face value. By the time he finally left school, he had been transformed from a sieve into a solid, worthy vessel.

People like Tom are victims of what I call the Sieve Syndrome. Children in this predicament may seek to be "filled" first through a desperate searching for compliments or ego-stroking that somehow never seems to satisfy. When the verbal attempts to fill them up fail, they may turn to a series of sexual relationships, destructive friendships, drugs, or other unproductive behavior. Yet, no matter how hard they try to find satisfaction through these means, they fail. The good feelings they experience quickly slip away, and often, they end up worse than they were in the beginning. Needless to say, when a teenager is in this mode, it's impossible to have a productive conversation with him.

Antidotes to this condition must begin with confronting the child about his condition. Just say something like, "You're being needy." Or, "You're being a sieve." In addition, it may help to provide extra parental support and companionship—though mothers and fathers must be careful not to allow this additional attention to feed back into the Sieve Syndrome and reinforce it. In a number of cases, it's helped children to receive positive feedback from parents and other adults about the youngsters' strengths and achievements. Also, this type of child is often open to instruction in how to receive and enjoy compliments.

Zelda's negative narcissism   Thirteen-year-old Zelda had grown faster than most of her classmates, had developed a mild case of acne, and in general was feeling quite unsure of herself. Both her parents had quite accurately pointed out that she was naturally pretty, had a good figure, and undoubtedly would be regarded as *very* attractive in a year or so when her peers caught up to her in height.

Part of Zelda believed her parents. But another part wasn't so sure. So she fished for compliments by using a ploy that I call "negative narcissism." She would say something like, "I know I'm really pretty ugly."

Then her mother would respond, "You're not ugly at all."

"Oh, yes I am. People look at me funny because I'm so tall, and I have these zits on my face."

Unfortunately, her parents didn't cut off these interchanges with a direct statement that Zelda *was* attractive but that it was also up to her to accept that fact. Instead, they just kept playing her game, even though no one, least of all Zelda, found the parental responses to be very satisfying.

Finally, Zelda began to look for more satisfying compliments and reassurances elsewhere. She began dating a strong-willed boy who soon talked her into a sexual relationship. She acquiesced because she saw sex as the trade-off for the boy's expressed admiration of her.

But as often happens in these teenage romances, the boy hadn't entered into the arrangement with any idea of a long-term commitment. Soon, another girl caught his eye, and Zelda was left to fend for herself. Before long, she was involved in another sexual liaison, and predictably, in a matter of a few weeks, she had broken up again.

The word of her behavior got back to her parents via a concerned teacher who had overheard some other students talking about Zelda's "problem." There were plenty of tears and angry words that flowed out of their confrontation over this issue. But fortunately, both the parents and the teenager were ready to talk about the situation.

Eventually, some counseling sessions helped the parents understand that among other things, Zelda was a victim of low self-esteem—or in my terms, the Sieve Syndrome. Although her parents had meant well, they hadn't responded in a way that convinced her she was really a worthwhile, attractive person. As a result, she had looked elsewhere for emotional satisfaction. Yet the sexual relationships had failed to provide an adequate substitute for parental commitment and love.

Both the mother and father in this family began to spend more time with Zelda, but this solution wasn't easy. This family, like most others, had developed firmly established patterns of interacting. With five children, there just weren't enough hours in the day to spend much time with any one child.

Still, both mother and father have done their best. The father now spends at least one hour alone with Zelda each week at a local coffee shop; and the mother makes time for several in-depth conversations each week.

So far, their efforts appear to be paying off. Now Zelda seems to feel more appreciated, largely because her parents are responding to her with real, honest thoughts and observations, not superficial compliments. She has more of a sense that her parents are aware of her problems and are rearranging their busy schedule to deal with them. Most important of all, they're all getting to know one another better. Zelda is no longer a "sieve" and appears to be well on the road to emotional recovery.

Secret #6: Daughters Need Mothers, and Sons Need Fathers

In the current cultural atmosphere, much is made of interchange-ability between the sexes. Women can hold men's jobs, and men can hold women's; both men and women can play the same sports; both are supposed to share household responsibilities. Also, with the rise of so many single-parent families, mothers (or fathers) often have to become two-parents-in-one for their teenager.

Yet, despite these trends, I believe firmly that there is a special importance in same-sex relationships between mothers and daughters, and fathers and sons. Without these relationships, or some substitute that fulfills a similar function, it's hard for children and parents to experience the full range of intimate talking relationships.

My reasoning? In order to function effectively in the adult world, we need good role models to show us how to behave and react. To be sure, you can learn a great deal from the parent of the opposite sex, and in some cases, you may learn all you need to know. But in *most* cases, there's no real substitute for a good same-sex role model to give a child the best chance at complete and well-balanced emotional development.

Perhaps the most important lessons we learn from our same-sex parents are how to relate both to people of the same sex and also to those of the opposite sex. Thus, sons need a strong male role model to learn how men deal with each other and with women. Similarly, daughters need a strong female model to understand how women relate to each other and to men.

Here are a couple of pertinent family situations I've encountered:

The daughter without a mother   Barb, a sixteen-year-old, had gotten into the habit of sleeping with every boy she dated the first time they went out. After the girl had contracted her third case of sexually transmitted diseases, her mother finally came to me visibly upset.

"It's going to be AIDS next," she said. "I just know it's going to be AIDS."

In the ensuing conversation, this woman revealed that she had little intimate interaction with Barb. In fact, this mother had almost no interaction because she was spending most of her time with her own mother.

"I call my mom two or three times a day, and I probably see her three or four times a week," she said, giving no indication that she felt there was anything wrong with this relationship.

"And how much time do you spend with Barb?" I asked.

"Well, after all, she's away at school. And when she comes home on vacations or weekends, she has her own interests."

In other words, she didn't spend any time with her daughter. So I proceeded to point out the fact that Barb was, in effect, a daughter without a mother. Furthermore, this mother spent very little time with her husband. Consequently, Barb had no example of how a mature woman could relate to her *or* to a man. In addition, the mother had no close peer relationships among other women her age. So again, Barb lacked a role model for establishing friendships with other teenage girls.

During our sessions together, this mother came to realize that there was something seriously wrong about her relationship with her mother. A grown woman, now in her forties, who had to stay in touch with her mother to the exclusion of her daughter and husband, was obviously in some emotional trouble.

So we began to explore ways that she could break away from this dependence on her mother and establish better ties with her daughter, her husband, and also female peers. It wasn't easy to make this transition. This mother felt guilty about "abandoning" her mother, as she put it. Also, she had trouble finding other women with whom she could talk.

It was especially difficult to break through the barriers that had separated her from her husband and daughter. After all, even though they liked the idea of deepening their ties with her, they had developed their own means of coping and conducting their lives. To pull her into their orbit meant making significant adjustments.

But over a period of several months, the attempts by this mother to enter the lives of her daughter, her husband, and her peers succeeded. As a matter of fact, she first made important changes with her peers by joining a small support group at a local church with women her own age. Although she had been invited to join this group more than a year before our meeting, she had declined. But the members were still willing and able to incorporate her into their sessions.

Also, she and her husband began to reestablish their relationship by going out on occasional "dates." As for Barb, the mother made more time available just to chat and muse in the daughter's presence. They planned outings and meals together, and spent much more time discussing things on the telephone.

The grandmother, by the way, who had been doing most of the talking on the phone with the mother in the past, felt somewhat neglected and miffed at first. But she soon adjusted to the new pattern in the family relationships and found other companions and interests to occupy her.

Although things are going much better with this family, I don't want to convey the impression that their situation has become some sort of miracle story. There are still plenty of problems.

Barb is learning a great deal from her mother now about how to relate to her peers and to men; but the teenager still periodically gets into unwise relationships with boys. At least now, though, she feels freer to go to her mother with her questions and concerns.

Also, the mother sometimes falls back into the habit of spending too much time with her own mother; and the husband has found it's not easy to alter his priorities and schedule to go out with his wife as often as she would like. But the situation in this family is definitely brighter than it was originally.

The son without a father   Actually, twelve-year-old Cal has a father, but for a long time, the family interactions were such that the father almost seemed invisible or absent.

From outward appearances, Cal's father in many ways projected the image of the all-American dad. He had sometimes shown up at Little League games and other sports events and was usually home in time for dinner every evening. On weekends, he even accompanied the family on many outings.

But this father rarely talked to his son about anything that really mattered. Certainly, they might chat briefly about Cal's performance in an athletic contest. Also, there would be the necessary "administrative" or "logistical" language that goes on in every family: "Cal, have you mowed the lawn?" Or, "Cal, turn that music down, please."

But for the most part, there was little intimate conversation between this father and son. They never discussed Cal's worries about his performance at school or in sports; or his doubts about his future; or his concerns about sex or peer relationships.

In short, this father provided his son with little guidance about how a mature man handles his inner feelings, relationships, and life-changing decisions. The sports talk and other superficial conversation had become an inadequate substitute for *real* talk between a father and a son.

One thing that signaled a problem might be developing in this family was that Cal had become quite uncommunicative and secretive. At first, this mother and father chalked this taciturn trend up to the onset of adolescence and Cal's need to become more independent. But then, they began to worry that he was becoming overly sullen and might be involved in drugs or some other harmful activity.

In fact, Cal was just feeling isolated both from his family and from his peers. He desperately needed intimate contact, yet he had trouble finding a group of friends with whom he was really compatible. Also, at this point he wasn't particularly interested in girls, and so he had no opportunities for relationships in that area.

This family identified their problem and began to change the family interactions at just the right time, before Cal began to "act out" in dangerous or unwise channels of activity. In the process of transformation, the most important—and difficult—part of the family's change occurred in the relationship between Cal and his father.

I recommended that the father set up situations where he and Cal *had* to talk and relate on a deeper level than in the past. Predictably, the father didn't feel at all comfortable at first. But as I explained, that was the point! He was *supposed* to feel uncomfortable because before, he hadn't engaged in any intimate discussions with his son.

"It's easy to remain guarded and protected when you're talking about how to catch or hit a baseball," I said. "But when you begin to talk about how you *feel*—your fears, doubts, and worries—that's something else. It's hard to be open and transparent about such things. And it's also difficult to give advice and guidance and ongoing support to a young person."

Fortunately, Cal's father was willing to be uncomfortable for a while in order to rebuild a good relationship with his son. As with Barb in the previous example, things aren't by any means perfect in this family. But Cal and his dad have made significant strides in strengthening their relationship and their ability to talk intimately with one another.

Finally, let me provide a word of encouragement to single parents. Obviously, if you're a mother who is rearing a teenage boy by yourself, you don't have the option of providing a father as a role model for your son. Still, there are powerful substitutes you can find if you make the effort. Here are a few that have worked in single-parent families I've worked with:

- The single parent can instruct the child of the opposite sex about how "good men" or "good women" behave in different situations. If you have an open relationship with your child, he'll trust you and probably incorporate most of the advice you give him in his value system.

  But obviously, this approach requires the single parent to do her homework about how an ideal parent of the opposite sex might respond. Also, it takes a great deal of time and patience to pursue these conversations and answer all the child's questions.

- The single parent can arrange outings with upstanding men (or women) to enable the child to establish friendships with these people and develop role models.

- Organizations like the Scouts, religious-school classes, or athletic teams can provide good adult role models. But be cautious and check out the adult leadership to be sure these are the kind of people you really want to expose your child to. Some adult leaders make wonderful role models, but others may have serious emotional problems or may espouse values that are opposed to your own. Research and observation are the only ways to make a wise choice in these situations.

Secret #7: Parents Should Celebrate Their Own Shortcomings

It's my impression that *every* parent has some pathology—some serious personal shortcoming—which may influence a child to become "unusual" or "abnormal" or even "maladjusted." Yet, even though parents often worry excessively about their own flaws and inadequacies, they fail to realize that it's these very problems that may ultimately result in a child's success. Paradoxically, it may even be appropriate to *celebrate* your shortcomings as a parent—at least up to a point!

I've already mentioned how my own parents' strengths *and* weaknesses shaped my caretaking ability. I'm sure I would never have been a counselor and educator of teenagers with special emotional problems if I hadn't been exposed to my particular home influences. Similarly, many accomplished people I know have reached a high level of achievement not in spite of, but apparently *because of* a special quirk, compulsion, or monomania they acquired from their parents' influence. Here are a few cases in point:

- One successful actor believed that his most important quality was the ability to overcome rejection. In the early part of his career, he was rejected constantly at auditions. But he stuck with it and finally began to get parts that eventually led to recognition and financial reward.

  How did he learn to overcome rejection? Probably there were a variety of factors, including native resilience and environmental influences he couldn't even remember.

  But one factor he *could* remember was that his family had moved around a great deal when he was young. As a result, he found himself frequently entering new schools or neighborhoods where he was always the outsider. None of the other children embraced him readily; so he had to find ways to overcome the initial rejection, push into their cliques and try to become "one of the guys."

It may be an overstatement to say that these circumstances were created by the pathology of the parents. But certainly, this boy found himself in environments that were created by the decisions of the parents to move. Furthermore, Mom and Dad never planned their relocations with an eye to the challenges or difficulties that their son would face in the new places.

In any event, this boy somehow found the inner grit and drive to meet the lack of acceptance head-on and survive the challenges with aplomb. And he's convinced, as am I, that his early experience in overcoming rejection was a key force in helping him persevere later in one of the toughest of careers.

- A prominent lawyer was constantly put down and abused verbally by a sharp-tongued father when he was a child. But he learned to stand up for himself and argue effectively with his father. As a result, he became a devastating debater in high school and college, and eventually a highly effective trial lawyer.

- A girl frequently received mixed messages from her parents: One would tell her it was all right to go out with friends on a school night, but the other would require her to stay at home. Or one would say, "If you'll do that chore, I'll give you a dollar," while the other would say, "That's the kind of chore you should be doing for nothing."

These conflicting communications caused her considerable anxiety at first. But eventually, as she got older, she became frustrated and even angry. "Why can't you get your views straight?" she'd complain. "I don't know whether I'm coming or going sometimes in this house."

While learning to function in this household, the girl developed a decided intolerance for confusion. She began to enter into the instructions and directives from her parents and helped make them consistent and shape them into clear, intelligible guidelines. Eventually, this skill she acquired in cutting through confusion helped her become a hardheaded, clear-writing journalist.

• An overprotective mother who constantly interfered in her child's athletic endeavors, school activities, and extracurricular involvements finally drove her son to tell her, in no uncertain terms, "Mom, I don't want you to stick your nose in this! I want to operate on my own!"

Granted, some children might have become overly dependent on such a mother. But this boy headed in the opposite direction and asserted his independence unequivocally. He became even more assertive and self-assured than most of his peers, and eventually, he moved on to become a promising junior executive in a major corporation.

As I mention such cases as these, however, let me offer a caveat: I don't want to suggest that in all or even in most cases a parent's flaws will positively influence a child's future. At best, that interpretation would be simplistic; and at worst, it might be dead wrong.

In the first place, some children with disturbed or seriously inadequate parents may be hamstrung in their ability to achieve anything as adults. Serious cases of sexual abuse or homes where one or both parents emphasize the idea that the child is totally worthless may fall into this category. The parental pathology in such situations may be just too much for the child to handle.

But these children whom I've cited had the emotional toughness and fortitude to turn difficult situations to their advantage. In effect, their parents' shortcomings ended up helping them later in their careers.

What lesson does this final secret have for you? Just this: Of course, you shouldn't be complacent about your weaknesses as a parent, nor should you be remiss in looking for ways to improve your relationship with your child.

On the other hand, one thing is absolutely certain: No matter how hard you try or how many children you have to hone your expertise, you'll *never* become a perfect parent. You'll always possess certain shortcomings or pathological tendencies which will cause wounds or discomforts in your interactions with your son or daughter.

So the best approach with your kids is just to relax and assume you'll fall short in some ways. Yet at the same time, be assured that even as you fail to live up to your parenting ideal, your child has important resources for overcoming your inadequacies and turning them to his or her advantage.

So long as you love that son or daughter and keep lines of communication open, you have a right to expect that your teenager will turn out all right. In fact, I expect that you may even eventually learn to celebrate your shortcomings!

PART II

Breaking Through to Different Types of Kids

CHAPTER 5

The Relationship Addict

The teenage years are a time when children develop a need for an increased amount of nurturing involvement with their peers, and especially with those of the opposite sex. The love and acceptance they received—or failed to receive—from their parents must now be transferred to companions their own age.

If the child has lacked satisfying ties with parents, it's likely that he will attempt to fill that void in various ways with peers. In fact, the desire for intimate human contact becomes so strong that the teenager may become what I've termed the Relationship Addict.

The Relationship Addict comes to depend heavily on peer-friendship attachments and emotional bonds. Because the sex drive often becomes overwhelming in adolescence, it's also likely that the child's expression of the need for love and acceptance will be sexual. In most cases, the involvements will be with the opposite sex, though sometimes a child with a deep need for parental attention and love may seek fulfillment in homosexuality. Yet at the root, the Relationship Addict's main need is not for the sex but rather for the warmth and understanding that the intimacy of sex seems to offer.

What are some of the signs that a teenager may be a Relationship Addict? Here are a few possibilities:

- The child has a deep need to have a regular dating relationship with a member of the opposite sex.
- She is sexually promiscuous.
- He is an active homosexual, or at least has a strong orientation toward same-sex relations.
- She seems to have boys on her mind most of the time.
- He's constantly on the phone with his girlfriend.

Obviously, a teenager who is not addicted to relationships may display some of these characteristics. But the true addict will reveal himself by indulging in such behavior far more often than the average child.

Your challenge, as a parent, is first to identify the addiction for what it is. Then, you must respond to it in such a way that you show your love to your child, and at the same time adjust your behavior so that your child has an opportunity to break free of the addiction to which he has become enslaved.

How Allison Broke Free

Allison, a fifteen-year-old Relationship Addict, had gone through a series of sexual relationships, beginning when she had just turned fourteen. She had already had sexual intercourse with five older boys, whom she had dated for varying periods, ranging from one month to nearly four months.

Her parents had been quite naive and oblivious to what was going on until they discovered her and her latest boyfriend in a state of undress in her bedroom when they arrived home early one evening. Then, all hell broke loose!

Allison's mother cried and hastened to attach blame: "How could you do this do us? Is this the kind of person you've become?"

Her father was even more accusatory and threatening: "You think I'm going to put up with this? This is a violation of family trust! Young lady, you're not going to leave this house until we get a few things settled!"

The boy ran out the front door, happy to escape with his skin. Allison retreated to her room crying, but also angry that her parents were "trying to run my life when you have no right to do that!"

Finally, after emotions had settled down, the three of them came together and continued their discussions in a somewhat heated and indecisive fashion. They eventually agreed to let a professional therapist try to sort through the mess in an effort to arrive at some kind of mutually acceptable solution.

During the counseling sessions, it became apparent that Allison was a classic Relationship Addict, one who needed ongoing relationships with boys to satisfy some unfulfilled need for love and acceptance in her life. The source of her problem seemed to be a deeply ingrained sense that neither her mother nor her father, both of whom held down high-powered jobs and often worked late hours during the week and on weekends, had much time for her or interest in her activities.

As is usually the case in such situations, both parents were shocked at this accusation. At first, they both denied they fit the picture that Allison was painting of them.

"We've always told her that we're just a phone call away if she needs us," her mother said. "And at least once a month, we try to get away to our country home. But frankly, as Allison has grown older, she seems more interested in spending more time with her friends than with us.''

All that was true. But it was also true that her parents were often quite distracted and preoccupied by their work concerns. They had rarely been physically present when she needed them as a child. So she had been forced to rely for emotional support on baby-sitters and other caretakers who weren't able to substitute adequately for Mom and Dad.

In short, Allison's relationship with her father and especially her mother left a great deal to be desired. Because of her lack of involvement with her mother, she had never learned how to relate properly to a member of the same sex—an ability which I've found to be a prerequisite to good relationships with the opposite sex.

The end result as she entered adolescence was to seek the acceptance of boys in an effort to find the love and acceptance she had received only sparingly at home. She became *obsessed* with trying to find a male who could give her the emotional nurture that her parents had not provided.

Furthermore, she focused on the *pursuit*, the striving toward a good relationship, rather than on the relationship itself. On the one occasion that she had dated a boy who seemed mature enough to build her up personally and emotionally, she abruptly ended the relationship before a sexual experience had even begun.

In most cases, the boys whom she chose were aloof, distracted, preoccupied, or less-than-completely committed to her —in much the way that her parents were. Also, whenever the relationship seemed to be settling down into a stable arrangement, she became restless and looked elsewhere for fulfillment. In short, she rushed off to find another boy, whom she fantasized could give her the intense and complete emotional satisfaction and bonding that she needed.

What could be done for a girl like Allison? Here's what actually happened:

The therapist knew that he couldn't "fix" the problems that she and her parents faced. They would have to take the initiative and do that themselves. But he *could* make some suggestions and guide them toward productive solutions.

First, he made sure that both the teenager and her parents understood that there really was a problem and that it was important to do something about it. That wasn't as hard as you might think, because the parents were thoroughly shocked by the revelations about their daughter's behavior.

As for Allison, she had been shaken by her parents discovery of her sexual activity, and she still genuinely wanted to establish better ties with them. More ominously, her father had even muttered something about "maybe having to send her away to a girl's boarding school"—and she definitely knew she didn't want that.

To be sure, she was angry and felt threatened that her independence was being curtailed. At the same time, she knew that her way of relating to her peers was not usual or normal for girls her age. She had no close girlfriends—a symptom of her inability to establish a good friendship with members of the same sex, including her mother.

All of her intense relationships were with boys, and those almost always involved heavy sex. From casual conversations she had picked up information that some other girls her age were engaging in sex. But she was also aware that she was having sex more often, with more boys, than any other girl she knew. Also, there had been whispers among some of her classmates that she was too "loose" or "promiscuous," and she didn't relish that kind of reputation.

Allison denied that she was "addicted" to relationships or sex when the therapist suggested this possibility to her privately.

But she did admit that she had some sort of problem and she knew that her parents weren't going to put up with her behavior much longer. So she was willing to try the therapist's approach, which began with a request that Allison keep a diary.

"Every time you even *think* about a boy, I want you to write that down in your diary," he said. "No one will be able to look at the diary—it's your private record. In fact, I want you to lock it up in a drawer, to which only you should have a key. And I'll tell your parents that they are expected to respect your privacy."

"Fine, but what's the point of a diary?" Allison asked.

"I want you to focus on how your mind is working, what's going on inside, motivating you. Just be honest, and bring your diary here with you for our session next week. I'll ask you some general questions about what you've written, and we'll both have a better idea of how to deal with this situation."

The therapist had arranged to see the entire family together for a session the following week. But he also set up meetings to talk to Allison and the parents separately, to enable them to feel freer to discuss their feelings outside the presence of the others.

When he next saw Allison alone, she had a strained look on her face. "This is too hard," she said. "Several days, it seemed that I spent all my spare time writing. My hand actually started to hurt. I still don't see the point."

"Think about it," he replied. "I suggested that you might be focusing far too much on boys. If you're doing that much writing, apparently I was onto something. What do you think?"

As she considered his observations, he could see a knowing expression come across her face. "I get it. Maybe I really *am* addicted to boys, or relationships, or whatever. I have to admit, that's almost all I was thinking about. Finally, I just quit writing so much, but I know I kept thinking about them."

During subsequent sessions, Allison continued to keep her

diary and soon went through a phase of hating herself. She really felt awful that she was gripped by this need to think about boys all the time. But the therapist just encouraged her to relax, continue to record her thoughts, and *accept* the fact that she was addicted or obsessed.

"That's the first step toward breaking free," he explained. "You recognize that you are addicted, and you also acknowledge that you're powerless to do anything about it. Then, paradoxically, you'll find that it's possible for change to begin to take place."

Sure enough, as Allison continued to keep her "relationship addiction diary," she found that it became less interesting to think incessantly about boys. So she began to record other feelings and insights, such as her concern about her grades and her friendships with other girls.

Also, the therapist moved more into the background and encouraged the parents to take over his role, as Allison's advisors. They began to adjust their busy schedules so that they could spend more time with her, and gradually they grew much closer to their daughter. The mother, especially, became more of a friend and confidante for Allison. In these ways, Allison was able to wean herself away from her obsession with boys.

In this particular case, a therapist played a key role in helping the teenager to break the addiction to relationships. But savvy parents could do the job just as easily—and at the same time deepen their own talking relationship with their child. The sequence of the "communication cure" might go like this:

- Identify the problem and raise the issue with the teenager, but *without* being accusatory or judgmental.
- Expect initial denial or resistance from the child, but realize that a large part of the problem has probably

been your own failure to establish a good talking relationship with your child.

- Suggest something like a diary to get the child to focus on his problem. Again, there may be resistance. But by far, the best way to overcome that resistance is to offer a positive reward—such as a discussion with you over a hamburger or as part of some other activity that the youngster likes.
- Once the teenager begins to confront his situation directly and consistently, the relationship addiction will most likely take care of itself. Other, more interesting and productive lines of thought and behavior will take over.

The emergence of a Relationship Addict from her bondage can be an exciting experience for everyone involved. I can recall one girl who became so enthusiastic about the new-found power over her life that she started a discussion group with several other girls with a relationship-addiction problem.

This response served two important functions: First, the girl was able to become the teacher and guide for other girls who were also admitted Relationship Addicts. Second, the group became a vehicle for all these girls to develop same-sex friendships—an important substitute for the hollow sexual relationships they had engaged in with various boys.

Of course, there may be many other complex issues that have to be resolved with a Relationship Addict. If a teenager is engaging regularly in sexual intercourse with multiple partners, that's dangerous, both physically and emotionally. So it may be necessary for the parent to set limits on whom the child can date—and require that first dates come over to the girl's home to meet Mom and Dad before they go out on the town.

In general, there's nothing wrong with such limits. They are necessary for the safety and also for the moral and emotional growth of the child. Furthermore, most children *want* lines to be drawn, even though they are sure to resist and push against those lines.

The challenge for parents is to draw lines that are realistic and reasonable. Also, they must devote the time and energy necessary to make it clear to the child that the limits of conduct are being set because Mom and Dad really *love* the child and desire what's best for him. Relationship addiction is hardly possible in homes where real intimacy and understanding exist between parent and child.

CHAPTER 6

The Weak Romeo

The Weak Romeo is a boy who typically is personable, is physically good-looking, and has no problem attracting girls. But he's not the classic "stud," the self-starting ladies' man or Romeo. Instead, he prefers to play a passive role with women: He expects them to make the first move—maybe even ask him out for a date—and also to take the initiative in seducing him.

To be sure, this kind of teenager enters willingly into sexual relationships and is almost never without at least one steady girlfriend. But he usually seems constitutionally incapable of establishing a solid relationship with anyone of the opposite sex. Furthermore, he has great trouble sharing deep feelings and thoughts with girls *or* parents, because he really doesn't know how to talk on a mature level.

Some typical behavior patterns and traits of the Weak Romeo:

- Girls tend to call him and invite him out on dates more than he takes the lead with them.
- He often seems unconcerned about or uninterested in

his girlfriends and rarely appears to think about them when he's not with them.
- He frequently lets his date determine what they'll do when they go out together.
- His mother probably makes most of the big family decisions and is the main parent who acts as guide for the boy's life.
- His father, more often than not, is a background figure in the family who provides little direction or input for the children.

The question for parents of a Weak Romeo is, "How can I really get through to my son in my discussions with him, and at the same time help him learn to become more assertive in his encounters with girls?" If a boy can begin to open up more, discuss his feelings with some candor, and then deal effectively with them, he'll automatically become more assertive in his relations with others.

Mark's Course in Emotional Muscle-Building

By his own admission, Mark was a "wimp" around girls. Certainly, he was by most measures a lady-killer; he never lacked for a date, and sometimes it seemed to his parents that girls were standing in line, waiting to go out with him.

All this might have been wholesome, innocent fun, and even a point of pride for his parents—except that the evidence was accumulating that his dates had turned into an ongoing round of sexual involvements. Among other things, they had discovered stockpiles of contraceptives in his room; and on two occasions, he had been treated for sexually transmitted diseases.

"So far, it's all been minor stuff that an antibiotic would take care of," his mother said. "But what happens when he gets

herpes, which won't go away? Or worse, I often wonder about
the possibility of AIDS.''

A counselor pointed out to Mark's parents that a major source
of the boy's problem could probably be traced back to his relationship with the two of them, the mother and father. Specifically,
the mother was the dominant spouse in the relationship and the
main force to be reckoned with in the family. Mark and his two
younger siblings always looked to her to make decisions for them;
their father was almost a shadowy figure who interacted little in
family disputes or discussions and for the most part, let his wife
run the show.

In fact, the mother was so strong that Mark and his brother
and sister were afraid ever to cross her openly. They knew there
could be severe consequences if they embarked on a direct rebellion against her authority. Her sharp tongue, willingness to
administer corporal punishment, and readiness to withhold privileges, such as allowances, were definitely forces they didn't want
to reckon with, at least not publicly. Instead, when they disagreed
with her, they made their opposition known more passively—
such as by ''forgetting'' to do something she directed them to
do, or by accomplishing the task late or in a halfhearted fashion.

This sort of family arrangement presents a difficult problem
for a boy and also for the parents, because a major shift in family
relationships is required to start the interactions on a course that
will help the boy. Things would have been easier if Mark had
been older and away from his parents' influence, or if he had
been guided independently by a strong therapist who could have
helped him become more assertive, regardless of what his parents did.

Fortunately, in initial meetings with a family counselor,
Mark's father saw the light and resolved to take a shot at helping
his son. This man, who was actually a fairly strong and aggressive

person at work, realized that he had in effect abdicated all direction of the family life to his wife. She had merely stepped into the vacuum created by his absence and was doing the best she could, given the fact that she was operating without a very helpful husband.

So Dad began to make his presence felt more in the home by taking over decision-making functions that he had neglected and also by interacting more with his children. His first order of business in this transformation was, as he put it, "to give Mark a little course in emotional muscle-building."

In a series of discussions with Mark about his love life, the father put these life-changing steps into effect:

Step 1   The father began to interact more forcefully with the mother—both to recapture some of his authority in the household and to give Mark a better role model for how men can interact effectively with women.

In taking this step, the father *didn't* try to overpower or demean the mother. That wouldn't have worked even if he had tried, because she was a very strong personality. Instead, he took the lead more often in family discussions and when reasonable and necessary, showed a willingness to engage in confrontations with his wife.

In short, this man moved from a passive to a more active role with the family in general, and with his wife in particular. As a result, without anything's having to be verbalized, Mark received a series of real-life illustrations about how healthier male-female relations should be conducted.

Step 2   The father, with the mother's support and assistance, encouraged Mark to assert himself more in relationships within the family, and especially in his interactions with his mother. He wasn't expected to be obnoxious or respond with abusive arguments to every request or suggestion. Rather, he was just given the green light to speak his mind when something was bothering him.

Step 3   In a series of father-son discussions, Mark learned that in the long run in a relationship, most women don't relate that well to weak men. "There has to be a balance between the man and woman for a relationship or marriage to work," his father told him. "I know I haven't been the best example for you, but believe me, I know what I'm talking about."

In fact, Mark really didn't believe his father at first. After all, most of what he had seen in marriage was his father's weakness and his mother's overpowering presence. On the other hand, he perceived some important, beneficial changes were taking place at home, and he was willing to accept the fact that these changes might have an important message for him as well.

Step 4   Finally, the father took the most difficult step in his son's "emotional muscle-building course." He encouraged Mark to try experimenting at being more forceful and assertive in his relationships with his dates.

"Look, I'll be up front with you," the father said. "You and I both know you've been treated for venereal diseases. That's dangerous stuff and could even threaten your life. You're a smart guy, and I know you know that. But have you ever considered that the reason you're getting these diseases is that you're allowing yourself to be pulled and pushed around by these girls? You're a good-looking, athletic guy, and you can bet that girls will always be after you. Unfortunately, though, the best girls will often hang back and be more selective, while the most aggressive ones may be the least desirable and even the most dangerous for you."

In effect, the father suggested that maybe Mark should check out some of the girls who played a little harder to get. Mark admitted that most of the girls he dated "aren't all that interesting. Actually, I don't even like most of them."

Underlying this observation, the father realized, was this unstated thought: "I may not like these girls, but at least they're easy to contact, they make all the decisions, and they're always willing to go to bed with me."

So the father emphasized, "These girls may be very available and seem to present relatively little trouble, at least at first. But how many of them are people you'd consider marrying? How many can hold your attention for a year or more? There's much more to a relationship with a woman than having her make all the decisions for you and maybe provide you with some exciting sex."

Now that he was really talking with his father for the first time in his life, Mark found he was more inclined to trust the man and listen closely to his advice. With this new-found respect, he discovered that he deeply wanted his father's approval. So he decided to try the suggestion that he date some of those girls who had caught his eye, but who had not thrown themselves at him.

The first time he picked up the phone to call one of these classmates, he experienced an unfamiliar emotion: fear. He found for the first time in memory that he was afraid of being rejected! When the girl accepted his invitation for a date, he breathed a huge sigh of relief—and enjoyed sharing the experience with his dad.

Then he ran into some unexpected challenges with a group of girls who sat on a class party committee with him. For the first couple of meetings, he had just occupied his seat passively, playing his usual nonassertive role. But now, feeling stronger as a person, he began to speak his mind on certain issues about the plans for the party—and he immediately met with opposition from the girls.

Mark's first reaction was surprise, because he couldn't remember ever getting into a real argument with a girl before, much less a group of females. Then, he got angry and lashed out, accusing them of being unreasonable and insensitive. The girls were stunned at this shift in his personality, but they held their ground and outvoted him and the other boy on the committee.

When Mark arrived home that evening, he was still rather upset. He could hardly wait for his dad to arrive home so that they could hash out the problem together.

"You've got to expect this sort of reaction when you exercise your personal power," the father said. "Not only that, it will take *you* some time to adjust your own response to girls you disagree with. Sometimes, you're going to get too angry, and other times, you'll fail to express your anger or dissatisfaction enough.

"Believe me, when you start dating some girl seriously and thinking about marriage, you'll find yourself disagreeing with her in a big way sometimes. But there's nothing wrong with that. The important thing is first to learn how to disagree. Then, you'll discover ways to compromise, and finally you'll find the relationship is growing stronger as a result of your disagreements."

As the father saw it, the spat at school was just part of Mark's training for showing anger and expressing disagreement—part of his "course" in becoming stronger in his relationships with women.

In this case, Mark's father was a fortunate man because he had first been able to identify his own problem with his wife and change his own behavior. Then, he was in a position to move to help his son alter negative behavior which he, the father, had been instrumental in creating.

Throughout their discussions, the father emphasized that Mark had to expect to make mistakes as he was changing his behavior and developing new personal skills. On occasion, he might become too angry or excessive, but that was all right. An apology can usually repair relationships that have been temporarily wounded, and some degree of freedom of expression is essential if we really hope to develop an understanding of one another.

In any case, a trial-and-error method is a necessary part of developing the capacity to communicate with anyone effectively. In essence, that's what *really* talking with your teenager is all about: first, being open about your feelings, and then working together to find ways of transforming both parent and child into more productive, powerful people.

CHAPTER 7

The Angry Child

Aside from love, anger may be *the* most common reaction parents get from their teenagers. Yet it's also the premier "hard-to-handle" feeling, both for the parent and the child. As a result, a furious outburst, or even a very controlled expression of rage, can become an extremely threatening and upsetting force in family life.

What is the current status of the "anger index" inside your adolescent? To get an idea of where your child stands, ask yourself how many times in the past week you've observed or experienced one or more of the following:

- An openly angry reaction of *any* type from your teenager
- A physical attack against you by your child
- A sense of personal fear that your child will lose his temper because of something you've done or something you're thinking about doing
- A threat by your child that she'll retaliate if you take certain action

• Expressions of anger by your child toward someone other than yourself
• Any malicious act by your child toward you or someone else
• Derisive or abusive remarks by your child toward you or someone else

If you've experienced or noticed even one of these responses, you're dealing with a child who is angry, at least to some degree. Of course, if the expressions of anger are limited—e.g., if they occur only occasionally and if they don't involve physical or extremely abusive verbal outbursts—that's quite normal. In fact, as we'll see shortly, a *failure* to express *any* anger may be as abnormal as throwing constant tantrums.

On the other hand, if your child completely loses control, becomes physically violent, frequently threatens to become angry, or often erupts in tantrums (say two or three times a week), then you may be dealing with the more serious Kid Type that I call the Angry Child. Over the years, I've noticed at least three main types of Angry Children: the Exploder, the Selective Attacker, and the Stifler.

THE EXPLODER

The Exploder is a child who simply can't control his anger. Like a human volcano, he periodically spews forth verbal or physical abuse—or engages in other offensive acts, like vandalism or stealing. In many cases, his behavior occurs in response to events or conversations that in no way seem to justify his outbursts.

Why does the Exploder behave this way? Often, the outbursts of anger are overflows of frustration because the child has been unable to get an appropriate reaction from the parent any other way. In short, the Exploder erupts because the parent has failed to talk!

One father, a self-absorbed investment adviser, spent every waking moment pondering financial strategies. Whenever he sat around at home, he would have a pencil, pad, calculator, and laptop computer near at hand. He rarely initiated a conversation with Lon, his fifteen-year-old son, or with his wife, though he was pleasant enough if they approached him.

Example: During a televised football playoff, the son and father were sitting in front of the TV. But though Lon was watching the action intensely, the father, as usual, was mostly paying attention to his investment notes.

A typical conversation would begin with Lon's saying something like, "Hey, Dad, did you see that? That was a great pass play. Fifty yards!"

Dad: "Yeah, nice"—though he never looked up from his calculator.

This interchange may seem typical of many families, except that the pattern occurred with unrelieved consistency between this father and son. Lon just couldn't break through and get a satisfying response from his dad, no matter how hard he tried.

The parents initially had become concerned because Lon began to lash out in loud shouting matches with both the parents, but especially the mother. The mother responded in kind to the boy, but the father reacted passively. He seemed immobilized by the rage Lon was expressing. The less the father reacted, however, the more the boy turned up the volume and intensified the insults.

Finally, this teenager turned his hostility toward the outside world. He became involved in several incidents of vandalism involving the breaking of car windows around the neighborhood. This destructive bent finally convinced the parents to seek counseling.

What was Lon's problem?

He was trying to get his father's attention. When he failed to secure a satisfying response from Dad, he escalated his attempts to communicate the only way he knew: He raised his voice. When that didn't work, he took the illegal action that he *knew* would make his father sit up and take notice.

The subconscious assumptions behind Lon's thinking actions went something like this: "I want Daddy to get involved in my life and show me what's right and wrong. Also, I want him to show me how to express my feelings. He's a man, and I need a male to give me an example I can follow. But there's something wrong here. I keep doing things to get Daddy to respond to me, but he *doesn't* respond. I think he loves me, and if what I'm doing is wrong, he would tell me. So I have to keep pushing harder and harder to find out where the line should be drawn between proper and improper behavior. But no matter how hard I push, he still doesn't respond to me!"

From the outside, this father may have seemed the ideal husband and parent, a good provider, and a reasonable, even-tempered dad. But in fact, his "even" temper was a symptom of a self-absorbed life and an unwillingness to show his emotions. Even more serious, this father's inability to respond adequately to his son caused the boy to become confused and angry. Lon felt he had to pursue bizarre forms of behavior to break through to his dad and get his attention.

Fortunately, in this case the father's problem wasn't a dislike of his son or a fear of confrontation. He was just naturally detached and *not* naturally interested in participating in the special activities or concerns of others, including those of his fellow family members. On the other hand, he did love his son, and when the counselor called attention to the boy's growing hostility and frustration, he responded by becoming more involved in Lon's life.

A teenage Exploder may also develop in a family where a parent—again, often the father—is *afraid* to stand up to the child's anger. One tough-as-nails entrepreneur was known for intimidating his employees with sharp retorts and rough verbal manhandling. But when he arrived at home after work, he changed personalities like some sort of human chameleon. He submitted totally to the control of Hope, his sixteen-year-old daughter.

Both the entrepreneur and his wife, who was a successful professional woman, organized their family activities and conversations so as to avoid any confrontations that might trigger their teenager's temper. Although Hope was shorter than her mother and only came up to her father's shoulder, all she had to do was glower at a suggestion she didn't like from her parents. In response, they would immediately back down or change the subject.

The situation deteriorated to the point that the girl was even able to control her parents at long distance. On one occasion, for example, she went away to a tennis camp during the summer.

"The food here stinks," she told them over the phone at the beginning of the camp. "Why didn't you check the menus before you sent me up here? I need some decent food, and I need it *now*!" Sure enough, the father was on the road the next morning with a package full of Hope's favorite snacks and dishes.

What gave this girl such dominance over her parents? There was a combination of factors. First of all, both mother and father felt guilty that they had to work such hard, long hours and had been unable to devote more time to their daughter.

Perhaps more decisive, both parents came out of family backgrounds where family members did all they could to avoid dealing directly with anger. The father's family had included a father who was quite abusive, both verbally and physically. He was an

Exploder, and his son—Hope's father—didn't want any more exposure to this kind of anger at home. In a sense, when he was at the office, Hope's father assumed an abusive role similar to the one his own father had played; but he reverted to a kind of gun-shy child when he was with his own family.

Hope's mother had also had a father who was known to have a terrible temper. But in this case, the anger rarely appeared, because the man fostered a fear that communicated this feeling in other family members: "I certainly wouldn't want to see what would happen if Daddy ever got mad!"

When all these influences were added up, Hope was magnified into a larger-than-life, fearful figure—a tiny girl to be sure, but one with whom nobody wanted to tangle. And she took advantage of this fact. She learned over the years *not* to say "please" when she wanted something. Instead, she just got angry or threatened to get angry. A red face, a hostile set to her lips, and a few high-decibel words were all that she usually needed to get her way.

Interestingly, it was the father's trip with the food to the tennis camp that pushed him and his wife over the edge. "We just can't go on like this," he said, and his wife agreed. But what to do?

They sought help from a family counselor who concluded after only one session, "I'll bet Hope never really gets angry!"

"What do you mean?" the father asked, certain that the therapist had completely missed the point.

"I'll bet Hope doesn't even know *how* to get angry. Chances are, her anger is all *affective* anger—that is, it's on the surface; it's make-believe. In a sense, she's play-acting at being enraged because she knows that will cause you to give her what she wants."

Further discussions revealed that Hope was on medication to overcome bouts of depression. "You know, depression is really repressed anger," the counselor pointed out.

In short, Hope put on a facade of anger to dominate and manipulate her parents; but she had never learned from her mother and father, her main models for behavior, how to express *genuine* anger. So the *real* anger became buried deep inside her, only to surface later in the form of depression.

The answer for this family was somewhat more complex than the solution for Lon and his parents. Among other things, Hope's mother and father had to learn two interpersonal skills that had eluded them for most of their lives.

First of all, they had to gird themselves to confront Hope directly, eyeball-to-eyeball, *every* time she exploded or threatened to explode in anger. The girl had been conditioned to expect that when she displayed outward signs of anger, she would get what she wanted. Now it was necessary to *de*condition her: She had to be shown that glowering, shouting, or throwing a tantrum wouldn't be a ticket any longer to *anything*.

Second, Mom and Dad had to begin to go through the difficult process of learning how to feel and express anger appropriately themselves. That wasn't at all easy, because both had developed the facility for bottling up their rage and avoiding confrontations. But it was clear that if they didn't learn how to handle anger in a healthy way, their daughter, who looked to them for guidance, probably never would either.

This family is still going through the process of transforming their distorted and repressed angry feelings into emotional expressions that are sounder and more constructive. In many ways, they still have a long way to go: Hope continues to fall back on affectations of rage. And occasionally, both the father and mother will be taken in and give her what she wants—just to avoid any possible unpleasantness.

But increasingly, the parents are standing up to their daughter. The teenager, in turn, is learning gradually how to express her wishes and argue her points without exploding.

THE SELECTIVE ATTACKER

Sometimes, a teenager will choose one or more "safe" people as the target for his anger but will shy away from expressing anger toward a person who is perceived as "unsafe," or more uncertain or volatile in his responses. This kind of Angry Child is an example of what I call the Selective Attacker. Here's how this situation may work:

In many divorced families, the parent who is the main caregiver for the children (in most cases, this is the mother) becomes the "safe" parent who receives the brunt of the child's pent-up rage. I call this adult "safe," because the youngster knows from experience that he won't lose this parent, no matter what abuse he heaps on her.

On the other hand, the absent parent is "unsafe" because, after all, he's already left the family to set up a permanent residence elsewhere. If the child displays too much hostility or other negative emotions in this parent's presence, he may disappear altogether.

Barton's father left home when he was only seven years old, an age when boys often begin to develop special attachments with the male authority figure in their lives. After the divorce, the father had visiting rights, and he occasionally showed up for Little League and soccer games. Those were precious times for Barton, because he could in effect show his friends, "Hey, I've got a dad, too!"

His father wasn't always on time to these events, however, and sometimes he didn't show up at all. In fact, he missed Barton's ninth birthday party, including the trip that had been planned to a professional baseball game. As you might expect, Barton was more than disappointed at these lapses in his father's commitment to him; he really became angry. But the anger was never expressed consciously toward his father. Instead, when he did get mad, Barton vented his rage against his mother, his friends, or anyone else in range.

Typically, he would shout at his mother about trivial or imagined offenses she had committed. Or he would provoke another child in the neighborhood and get into a fight. But *never* did he lash out at his father, who was the real source of his anger.

The reason? His mother was a "safe" person, whom he knew from experience would always be there for him, always ready to support him, no matter how terrible his behavior. Even the other children were "safe," because they always seemed available to play, even after he had pushed them around. But his father was "unsafe." Dad couldn't be relied upon to show up even for important events in his son's life; so it was logical to assume that serious anger might cause him to leave for good.

Barton's father never entered into the process of showing his son how to be angry in a healthy way. As a result, as he grew older, Barton's way of expressing anger became even more distorted. Typically, he would lose his temper with girls he dated seriously—a replay of those angry outbursts with his mother. But he couldn't assert himself with authority figures like teachers, coaches, or employers.

In consultation with a therapist, Barton, who is now eighteen, is learning better how to cope with his emotions. It's just too bad that he wasn't in a position to be taught these lessons by a more available and competent father.

THE STIFLER

In some families, there are emotions that are "not OK" to express, and anger is one of the most common of these. I sometimes say that there is an unwritten Eleventh Commandment that is taught to many kids: "Thou shalt not get angry at thy parents." This precept is communicated in a number of common ways:

- "We don't behave that way around this house."
- "You show respect for your mother!"
- "I won't hear that kind of talk, young man!"

Of course, it's necessary for parents to teach respect and to discipline children when they get out of line. But this instruction in being a good son or daughter shouldn't involve the complete elimination of open expressions of anger. In the first place, just or righteous anger has always occupied a revered place in healthy, productive relationships, from the words of the Old Testament prophets to social reformers who have advocated various forms of human rights.

Next, you can't get rid of anger even if you want to. By refusing to acknowledge it or by prohibiting it, you'll just cause it to go underground. That's how the Angry Child I call the Stifler makes his appearance.

This teenager has learned that when he feels anger, he must express it *not* in a normal, direct way—such as by raising his voice, speaking sharply, or just stating, "I'm angry about this," or "I'm angry at you." Rather, he has to stifle those normal channels of expression and show his anger through other means. Consider a few I've come across in recent months:

- Jack began to steal and deal in drugs, mainly to get his parents' attention. He had been told that it was unacceptable to express anger around the house, and when he did say something hostile to his mother or father, he would be hit or otherwise severely punished. Like a growing thirst that needed to be satisfied, Jack's anger finally drove him to other outlets. The hostility that he bottled up in him finally emerged outside the home in destructive, illegal acts.
- Trish was consistently nasty toward the boys she knew,

and understandably, few were interested in dating her. She developed a reputation for being a young woman who "hated men." Yet, her nastiness was nothing more than an expression of the years of anger that she had kept inside herself as a child, anger which her parents had taught her shouldn't be expressed directly.

• Don, whose parents are divorced, hasn't seen his father in five years. He explains, "Well, maybe he doesn't get in touch because he's embarrassed about having left us." Don is also known as a boy you "don't mess with," because he has a "short fuse."

Translation: Don is angry about his father's absence, and he's avoided direct feelings of anger toward dad by rationalization. But the rationalization isn't sufficient to eliminate the anger, which emerges from another spot in Don's personality in the form of a short temper.

• Carol frequently giggles and jokes when she talks about her personal problems, such as her mother, who committed suicide, or her ex-boyfriend, who recently jilted her. But in fact, the laughs are all a cover-up for the anger she feels toward her mother, her father (who is now caring for her and whom Carol blames in part for her mother's death), her former boyfriend, and even certain girlfriends, whom she feels have let her down. In fact, Carol is a very depressed girl, the depression being the primary expression of the anger that has been bottled up inside.

How do teenagers like Jack, Trish, Don, and Carol learn to deal with their misdirected anger in a healthier way?

In each of these cases, the available parent or parents are helping the young person to *flush out* the anger they harbor through normal channels. It's a matter of the parent's saying, in effect, "It's all right to get mad at me or anybody else at times."

Also, many of the parents must first learn to express their own anger. When the adults can accomplish this, their children automatically have a role model to help them in their own venting of emotion.

Of course, each family must set its own reasonable limits on the expressions of the anger. Physical abuse should always be ruled out. Also, most families elect to outlaw curse words or personal insults. Finally, a reasonable time limit and location is usually placed on the expressions of anger. In other words, the child can't be permitted to rant and rave at the top of his lungs for ten or fifteen minutes in the local restaurant. Still, the limits should provide ample leeway to vent deep, violent emotions in a safe environment, where feelings are adequately flushed out, but no one gets hurt or abused.

We have an exercise among our students that illustrates graphically how a person who has been unable to express anger can learn how to express and experience this important emotion safely. First of all, I identify the Stifler, the boy or girl who is having special problems showing anger. Then, with his or her permission, we pick eight to ten other students to hold the Stifler down.

"OK, now you can be as angry as you like," I'll say. "I *want* you to get angry. Yell, thrash about, let it all out."

It's amazing what sometimes happens after that. The amount of energy pent up inside these kids can be amazing. It actually does take all the eight to ten children acting as "holders" to restrain the Angry Child. Yet, when the exercise is finished, the Stifler has usually made great strides toward understanding and resolving his problem.

In a family context, the closest analogy I can think of to this exercise is the parent's holding the child who is having a tantrum. The mother or father will let the child have a good "run" at getting rid of those deep, hostile feelings. Then, the parent may finally say, "OK, that's all right. That's enough. Let's cut it out now!"

The Angry Child, in all his varieties, is one who has never learned how healthy anger should fit into everyday life. So the parents' goal should be to show this child the *appropriate* outlets to display anger.

Parents have a responsibility to let kids know it's *not* all right to express anger indefinitely or in public places where other family members may be embarrassed. Nor is it acceptable to hurt others, either physically or psychically, with your hostility. But it *is* all right to show anger directly in many situations. Moreover, these direct displays of anger are absolutely essential for the emotional health of children and for the family life of parents who want a full talking relationship with their teenagers.

CHAPTER 8

The Runaway

Running away from home is perhaps the most obvious way of breaking lines of communication. But how should we define running away?

Among our students, running away means going off grounds without permission. Whether it's for five minutes or five days, the child who is "absent without leave" is regarded as a runaway.

At home, the definition will vary according to the rules you want to set up. In most cases, parents will probably want to posit a general time limit of no more than twenty-four hours for regarding their teenager as missing or a runaway. With some families, this time period may be considerably shorter, depending on how often the child *usually* checks in with parents about his whereabouts.

RUNNING AWAY IS AN ALL-FAMILY PROBLEM

The way the entire family operates in practice will provide some pointers to a meaningful definition. For example, husbands and wives have sneaky ways of running away, such as by staying late at work. Although this sort of behavior may never be labeled explicitly as running away, the child gets the message that Daddy or Mommy is behaving in a "runaway" fashion, and he may begin to model his own behavior along the same lines.

But because parents often don't understand the significance of what they are doing in their marital relationship, they may also miss the point of what the child is doing. They won't understand that when a child disappears for a while, he may just be saying, "Like Dad, I have to take a breather from this family."

So with a runaway problem, it's important to get each member of the family to examine his own feelings and behavior and recognize it for what it is. When parents do this, the actions of the child will become more understandable.

A related issue is the teenager who "runs away" from the family in more socially acceptable ways but is never called to account for it. For example, a boy may attend stamp club after school, then spend some time in the library, and arrive home just in time for a quick supper. Finally, he'll spend the rest of the evening in his room doing homework. In fact, his overall behavior may be a form of running away, but it's never seen as such. Ironically, the child may even be praised for this conduct!

I understand that any parent would be less worried about this studious stamp collector than about the boy or girl who leaves town for several days or a week without permission. There are immediate dangers that threaten this second kind of runaway, such as drugs, prostitution, or other physical perils. But in fact, *both* types of withdrawal have serious implications for purposes of effective parent-child communication. And in every case, something negative is going on in the family or in the child's life which triggers the leave-taking.

WHAT DRIVES SOME KIDS AWAY

Ron Ironically, a fifteen-year-old boy, Ron, ran away from our campus *after* he began to improve his grades and other students started to regard him as a potential leader. He had never felt so successful, and he fled because he didn't know how to handle these great feelings. He was scared. He didn't know how he had moved up to this position, and he wasn't able to sort out all the good things that were happening to him.

So Ron actually traveled to another city, lied about his age, got a job in a fast-food restaurant, and soon become the assistant manager! In this new environment, he became successful, just as he had been successful at home—but he still felt as lonely and confused as he ever had. So finally, he called us and his parents, described where he was and what he was doing, and said he wanted to return to school and try to work things out.

Fortunately, the parents in this situation were relaxed and accepting. They didn't begin to accuse the teenager of doing something bad or ask, "How could you have worried us like this?" Instead, they saw that the boy's main problem was that he was confused and needed to work out some deep emotional problems before he could find some peace and a sense of equilibrium. The experience of running away actually helped Ron begin to confront his problems directly, because he now saw that the source of the difficulty wasn't his parents or his home or the school, but himself.

Chuck Some kids like Chuck are natural "runners." They run away often in an effort to resolve their personal problems.

Chuck's mother felt her main purpose in life was to take care of him, and nobody could do it as well as she could. She, as much as anyone, helped close him off from the rest of the world.

Yet, he also avoided talking to his mother on a deep level, because those conversations were quite disturbing to her. Whenever he did something wrong, such as skipping a class or getting into a fight—and he told her—she would become overwhelmed and distraught by his behavior.

So Chuck learned to hold in the things that really mattered to him. He couldn't talk to his mother; he didn't have a father around because his parents were divorced; and he didn't know how to reach out to anyone else. In effect, then, Chuck became a very lonely boy.

"I isolated myself by doing bad things and then feeling that I wasn't able to tell anyone about them. That made me feel very much alone," he recalled. "I set myself up to feel guilty about things I had done, but I was in a box, because I couldn't share my thoughts and feelings. The only thing I could do to relieve the pressure was to run away."

But after running away numerous times, Chuck finally recognized that "this wasn't getting me anywhere. I got involved in more problems when I tried to get jobs out of town or make friends away from home. I found I couldn't trust other people, and they wouldn't trust me. They couldn't count on me, because when something started to go wrong in my life, I'd just pick up and leave."

Chuck was prevented from running away several times when his mother discovered a packed bag in his closet. But more often than not, when he wanted to leave, he was able to leave.

Overall, though, the experiences he had weren't exactly liberating or high adventure. He ended up sleeping on the street many nights, going without meals, and in general, being very uncomfortable. Much like Ron, Chuck decided on his own that it was far preferable to live at home and try to work out his problems there with his mother—who was beginning to get some insights through counseling.

Gail Gail was in the habit of taking off from home every six months or so, sometimes for a couple of days and sometimes for more than a week. Typically, after she had been gone several days, Gail would call home and ask her parents to send her some money.

At first, they were so happy to hear from her, they complied immediately. But then, it dawned on them that they were in effect supporting Gail's runaway habit and preventing her from having to work through the issues that were driving her to flee. They were making it too easy for her to be a runaway!

A therapist working with this family agreed with the parents and encouraged them not to support the girl when she took off.

"If she's going to do this, she has to take full responsibility and go through the experience by herself," the counselor said to the parents. "The lessons she learns can't be contaminated by your money or goods. Gail really has to feel like she's on her own. That's the only way she can go through the loneliness that will provide her with the time she needs to experience inner healing."

The parents went along with this advice, even though the process was painful. When Gail took off on another occasion for several days, she called her parents to send her some extra clothes and wire her some money. But this time, they refused. "You're old enough to leave home on your own, and you're also old enough to take care of yourself when you make that decision," her father said.

Gail became quite angry at this response. But before long, she returned home again, and this time, she seemed able to relate to her parents more as an adult. Also, the parents became stronger in relating to Gail honestly, and overall, the relationships in this family improved immensely. Furthermore, the running away stopped because Gail no longer felt she had to leave home to solve her problems.

GETTING AT THE ROOT OF THE RUNAWAY PROBLEM

Regardless of the type of running away you've encountered, the way of dealing with it is similar. You can't physically force the teenager to remain at home, because that will just make him want to run more. Instead, you need to ask, "What's going on in this family that we don't know about? What's causing the child to act this way?"

It may be that the teenager is responding by fleeing physically because no one has ever shown him how to respond otherwise. In that case, it may be helpful just to sit down with the teenager, give him a chance to open up and talk about his problems, and show him ways he can deal with his difficulties other than by running.

Or there may be intense feelings and pressures in the family that no member is dealing with well. So the father runs away to the office; the mother runs away to her church activities; and the daughter runs out of town. In such circumstances, the parents must look at the family more closely and change the environment so that people want to stay together, rather than take off.

How do you change the family environment? The first step is to begin to talk to other family members, and especially the teenager, in as nonjudgmental a way as possible. In some non-threatening way, ask the youngster what goes on in her mind when she runs away. Try to get her to open up. Above all, don't criticize the runaway. Rather, probe to find out what's motivating her. What is she running from? Are other family members experiencing the same thing?

There has to be some two-way honesty in this discussion, too. You can't expect your child to open up to you if you don't open up to her. She may say, "I run away because Mommy nags me so much sometimes I feel like killing her!'' Instead of becoming defensive, Mommy should encourage her daughter to explain exactly how the nagging is occurring and what bothers the girl most. Also, a discussion like this will provide an opportunity for both of the parents to disclose what *they* don't like about the family situation, and perhaps what makes them run away as well.

Should you ever try to stop a child from running away?

Yes, I think in many cases the parent should try to head off an escape attempt because it really *is* dangerous out there in the hard, cruel outside world for an immature teenager. On the other hand, as I've indicated previously, using physical force or locking the child in her room won't work. Instead, it's necessary for the parent to give the teenager a chance to tell her side of the story and to offer suggestions about what changes might be made in the family or in herself to remedy the runaway impulse. In particular, the parent should try to understand that running is not primarily a hostile act toward the mom or dad. Instead, flight is the most comfortable thing the teenager can do at this point in time.

FROM SELF-BLAME TO BLACKMAIL

Many times when a kid runs away, parents think they have done something wrong, but that isn't necessarily so. Sometimes, when things get better in a family—for instance, when relationships become more intimate—the child may not know how to handle the closeness. So he flees instead of dealing with it directly.

Are parents responding inappropriately if they become depressed or emotionally traumatized by the child who takes off? This sort of reaction can distract parents from the real issue and may be counterproductive or even dangerous: Parents must keep a balanced, calm attitude if they hope to remain rational and be able to identify what the child has to do in order to return home and *stay* home.

So instead of focusing on the more constructive issue of how the kid needs to change, Mom and Dad may begin personal soul-searching in an effort to figure out what they have done wrong. In such a state, the parents become vulnerable to blackmail from the child. A typical attitude by the perceptive teenager, who notices a power vacuum in the family, may be described something like this:

Teenager: "I want you to get such and such for me."

Parent: "I'm afraid we just can't afford that right now."

Teenager: "Then I'll have to run away again."

Parent: "Oh, no, I couldn't handle having you on the road again."

The interchange isn't usually in quite such crass, obvious language, but this dialogue certainly reflects a common underlying message. Also, parents frequently give in and give their teenagers what they want in an effort to prevent further conflict.

Sometimes, very needy parents may be involved, who need the child more than they should. In this situation, running away gives the teen an opportunity to break from the family and get some breathing space. Of course, the separation that the child achieves is illusory. Even when he is miles away, he's still emotionally tied to the family, trying to live his life without having resolved any problems that arose when he was at home. In fact, if he were able to separate himself in a maturely independent way, he could as easily do that while living at home!

Usually, parents feel that if a kid runs away, he "doesn't care about us." But actually, the opposite is true. Most children run because they care deeply and can't stand the intense feelings of being trapped in an enmeshed family system. So in evaluating why a child runs, it's very important to evaluate just how and why the child is overwhelmed by the family relationships.

I know that it can be nerve-racking and frustrating to have a child run away. When any of the boys or girls on our campus takes off, it's always fingernail-biting time for me, as well as the parents. But if I've done all I can to prevent the flight, the best approach for me is to sit back and let the running away quite literally run its course. Ultimately, neither I nor any parent can put shackles on a teenager or put him behind bars. The child himself must discover that he is the one who must learn to resolve his fears and frustrations in a more constructive way.

Remember: Running away is never the problem; it's always a *symptom* of the problem. Your challenge as a parent is to probe and investigate and learn what the underlying difficulties really are.

CHAPTER 9

The Weird Dresser

One of the main ways that teenagers assert their increasing independence from their parents is to wear clothes, accessories, or hair styles that make a statement. The "looks" that are popular change from year to year, and even month to month. But as I write this, some of the styles that are either in vogue (or just going out of or coming into vogue) are these:

- Anything worn by the latest rock star
- Earrings for boys
- Multicolored hair and makeup for girls (or boys)
- Shaved sides of head, with designs or letters carved into hair
- Torn jeans
- Brassieres or other lingerie (including boxer shorts) worn by girls as outer attire
- Sneakers unlaced
- Never a tie or jacket (unless parents are against ties and jackets—then, the kid will most likely favor them)

These styles are not designed to make parents happy. For that matter, one of the purposes in wearing them is to startle and disconcert adults. The kid's apparel says, "I'm a separate person from my parents—and these clothes, which are so unlike theirs, broadcast my independence!"

WHAT TO DO ABOUT CRAZY CLOTHES

So how should Mom and Dad respond to outlandish dress?

I say, welcome it! This is one of those extremely safe family battlegrounds where gut-level conversation can occur and compromises can be made on both sides—without endangering the teenager's life or limb.

I realize, of course, that many if not most parents become agitated, disgusted, embarrassed, or all of the above when a daughter walks downstairs wearing a school outfit that would seem more appropriate for the local charity drive. But many teenagers have to go through the Weird Dresser stage as a personal rite of passage to adulthood. They need to make their sartorial statement as a way of saying, "I'm spreading my wings," and then they can feel free to move on to more normal attire.

So my first advice to parents with children going through this phase is *relax*! Be thankful that you're not dealing with drugs, promiscuous sex, or some other threat. It's even helpful to approach the situation with an attitude of fun and good humor. After all, some of these outfits are better than Halloween!

Second, I would suggest that parents remember the red rover game that we discussed in an earlier chapter. It often helps to play it with a vengeance when reacting to the Weird Dresser in your home.

Return to Red Rover

As you'll recall, the child's game of red rover involves dividing a group into two teams and having one representative of a team try to break through a line formed by the other team. The game is fun and vigorous, but quite safe if a child breaks through the opposing line. The most that will happen is that he may just tumble down on the grass before he returns to his own side with a "captured" player. On the other hand, if red rover were played on the edge of a cliff, there could obviously be big problems with breaking through the line!

It's the same way in family encounters and battles. If the dispute is over whether or not the child will use drugs, you're operating on the edge of a cliff. If the child "wins," he may be destroyed. But with issues of apparel, there's plenty of room for either parent or child to win or lose without dire consequences.

This point has been impressed on me at our campus, where we have a dress code that is always causing controversy. As it stands, we say kids can't wear torn jeans or other shredded clothes, nor can boys wear dangling earrings—though they *are* allowed to wear one single gold post in their left earlobe. If they violate the rules, they lose some privilege.

Now, these rules seem clear, don't they? But the kids constantly test our resolve. One boy made it a point to walk past me the other day wearing a gold loop in his ear instead of a post. I stopped him and asked, "What's that thing in your ear, Mac?"

"It's my gold earring, like you said we could wear."

"Sure. Just *when* did I ever say you can wear a gold loop?"

"Well, it's a small gold earring."

"It's a loop, not a post. Sorry, Mac. You lose your earring privileges."

"But a loop is practically the same as a post!"

"But they're *not* the same, are they?"

"Almost the same."

"How many times have you heard about the earring rule?"

"I don't know. I don't remember anything being said about a little loop. I thought that was okay."

"Come on! You know you're only allowed to wear a post! When have you ever heard differently?"

And so on, and so on. The voices may become a little loud and strident. Passions may even rise. But the battleground is safe.

In this case, I held my ground about taking away the earring privileges; but as I always do, I kept the time period for the suspension open-ended. When the teenager felt he was able to go along with the program we had set up, then he would be free to begin to wear an earring again. It had to be *his* choice, not just mine.

Earrings are a typical issue that we fight over at our school, though in the past, I've made mistakes and set up my "red rover lines" too near the cliffs of life. For example, years ago I stupidly allowed the teenagers to smoke cigarettes if they wanted to. As a result, when they wanted to rebel or assert their independence, they had to look beyond cigarettes to marijuana or hard drugs.

One girl tried a typical smuggling trick we've encountered a number of times. She took her stereo speakers home over one vacation and while she was away, she stuffed the speakers with marijuana. Another student did the same thing with tape cassettes—he opened them up and plugged in the grass.

But now, since we've moved our lines of acceptable conduct forward, they don't smuggle in grass or drugs as much as they do cigarettes! And of course, when we find the contraband, we'll make as much of a stink about it as we did with the drugs. But as you might guess, we heave a sigh of relief that we're not treading on more dangerous ground.

The main point is that teenagers often feel a need to break the rules and deal in banned substances and practices of one sort or another, whether it's cigarettes, drugs, or strange clothing. Parents *can't* prevent the rebellions or expressions of independence. But they *can* influence the fields on which those fights are fought.

A QUESTION OF POWER

In the last analysis, the issues raised by the Weird Dresser and his kin are issues of *power*. Part of growing up is learning to assert yourself and exercising power in relationships with other people, but without hurting yourself or the other person.

I'm reminded of Nan, the daughter of some *very* traditional, straight-dressing parents. The girl, a fifteen-year-old, insisted on wearing the strangest, most unattractive clothes and accessories I've ever seen. Basically, she was a rather pretty person, but she seemed obsessed with the idea of making herself look disheveled and unkempt. Her favorite attire, for example, was a long black dress, highlighted by scuffed men's leather shoes, green-flecked hair, green eye shadow, and black lipstick.

Why did this teenager dress this way? In part, it was because her peer group also wore unusual clothing—though her styles were by far the most radical. Even more important, Nan was trying to distinguish herself from her parents. But the key to this story is that Mom and Dad had resolved not to criticize or even respond. It's as though your best friend met you downtown for lunch wearing only his underwear, and you just said, "Hello, how are you today?"

Failing to get a reaction with her first attempt at Weird Dressing, this girl had escalated her drive to get a rise out of her folks. That's how she ended up being the most radical dresser in her peer group. Furthermore, she was already experimenting with drugs and sex, also in an effort to distinguish herself from her parents. The unspoken rationale: "You don't react when I wear strange clothes, so let's see what happens when I try drugs and sex!"

Nan's parents failed to realize that her Weird Dressing was a cry for instruction in values and the use of personal power. Nan knew that as she grew older, she had more power at her disposal. But where did it begin and where did it end? What was an appropriate use of new-found strength and independence?

By becoming a *very* Weird Dresser, she was pushing or nudging her parents to try to get them to show her how far she should go. Such pressure by a child on parents is a form of communication that asks, "What are the values I should observe in my life? What's helpful for me to do and what not? What are the consequences of some of these actions I'm taking?"

It was confusing and frustrating for her not to get any response at all when she came downstairs in a costume that even she sensed might be more befitting in one of the rings of a circus. Surely, she thought, my parents would let me know if I'm doing something stupid or hurtful. Yet I wonder why they don't show any reaction at all?

In the last analysis, the subconscious or even conscious conclusion that such a teenager may come to is, "I guess my parents don't care at all. Maybe they really don't even love me."

Of course, if Nan's parents had commented on her dress, they would have initially received a strong argument back from their daughter—and maybe even an explosion. Fearful of such a reaction, the parents elected to keep their mouths shut. Also, they rationalized, "Our relationship with Nan is more important than any clothes she might wear. This is just a phase she's going through, and so we'll be understanding and nonjudgmental and wait it out."

In fact, though, by *not* engaging Nan in a discussion about her dress, they were sending the girl the message that their relationship wasn't very important at all! Kids get angry and frustrated and may stamp off to their rooms when Mom or Dad resists or rejects some unreasonable teenage practice or desire. But after the dust has settled, the link between parent and child is usually stronger—that is, if the parents continue to demonstrate their love and if their decision has really been reasonable and in the child's best interests.

Adam's Lesson

Another kind of power issue may emerge during the actual confrontation between the parent and the Weird Dresser. Adam, a seventeen-year-old who was in the process of applying to various colleges, announced that he had an admissions interview that afternoon. About fifteen minutes later, he walked into the living room where his father was sitting after arriving home a little early from the office. But Dad did a double-take when he saw what the boy was wearing: an open-necked sports shirt, a wrinkled pair of wash pants, and a pair of sneakers.

"You're going to a college interview like *that*?" the father asked.

"Yeah. I decided to get dressed up."

"You're kidding."

"No, you saw what I was wearing when I came in from school, didn't you?" As a matter of fact, the father had noticed that Adam had been wearing an *older* pair of sneakers, a pair of jeans, and a T-shirt. So, arguably, he was more dressed up now than he had been before. But that wasn't enough to convince the father.

"Adam, you really should wear a coat and tie. After all, you're trying to make the best impression."

"I never wear a coat and tie to anything, Dad. Besides, this isn't that important an interview."

"So why go? Why waste your time? On the other hand, if you think there's any chance you *may* attend this school, you should give it your best shot in the interview as well as in the rest of the applications process."

The discussion continued for several more minutes, and finally, Adam reluctantly conceded and went back to his room to change into something more appropriate.

What was the power issue in this exchange? Adam not only got some important instruction in making a good impression in an interview; he also received some essential practice in defending a personal decision he had made. His father saw he was making a mistake and called him on it.

In this case, the father would ultimately have allowed the son to go ahead to the interview dressed in any way he liked. But he wouldn't let him go without first providing him with the benefit of some wise advice. Fortunately, Adam, in taking that advice, learned something about the limits of his own power (he could exercise it in this case, but not without being challenged). Also, he was given a chance to evaluate his initial decision, to defend it, and finally to change it under the barrage of more compelling arguments.

Through such encounters as these, parents can help Weird Dressers—and teenagers who are asserting their independence in other ways—to understand and use the growing power that they are gradually acquiring. Weird Dressing is just another way of saying, "Hey, I'm my own person!" but at the same time asking, "How do you think I'm doing in my development?"

Parents usually recognize the first point—that strange dress is a way of asserting independence. But they often fail to answer the unspoken question about their opinion of their child's decisions and development. Teenagers desperately need feedback from their parents at every step of the way. Only then will it be appropriate for Mom or Dad to step back and allow the youngster freedom to spread his wings and fly.

CHAPTER 10

The Wild Child

Some teenagers seem totally out of control. They move from outburst to outburst, disobedience to disobedience, or even crime to crime, almost without pause. Others have occasional wild episodes or binges, which seem to be triggered by no particular cause, other than a buildup of passions that must be vented at periodic intervals.

This sort of youth, whom I call the Wild Child, can drive parents to distraction. But interestingly enough, the child who loses control or who consistently engages in socially offensive behavior is usually just trying to get his parents' attention and provoke some sort of response.

These kids accomplished the same thing when they were preschoolers or elementary school students by throwing a tantrum, damaging furniture, getting into fights, or doing other obnoxious acts. Now, the same youngsters resort to more upsetting or even dangerous forms of "acting out."

There are many reasons why certain teenagers become Wild Children, but four kinds of individuals have struck me as especially vulnerable to the Wild Child syndrome: the passive kid; the kid who cares too much; the kid who feels empty inside; and the kid with parents who like to be abused.

THE PASSIVE KID

Frank, a very sensitive fourteen-year-old, had a wild side to his nature. He periodically got involved in pranks or acts of mischief with his buddies, such as decorating a neighbor's flower garden with toilet paper or soaping up the windows of a friend's family car.

But then, he went too far. One evening at the local movie, while waiting for the next feature to begin, Frank and two friends damaged a video game in the theater lobby by rocking it back and forth. The manager and a couple of ushers cornered them and called the police. The boys' parents managed to talk the movie people out of pressing charges by promising that they, the parents, would pay for a new video game.

At the same time, however, Frank's mother and father knew that this was not the end of the story. Clearly, something had to be done to deal with the wild streak in their son. A counselor helped the parents and the boy work through the situation this way:

First of all, both the parents and child had to understand the complex factors that were driving Frank to behave as he did. A series of therapy sessions—which really amounted to nothing more than in-depth discussions about the feelings of the family members—revealed that there was one overriding characteristic to Frank's personality: He was a rather passive person, who somehow "fell into" bad behavior when he was hanging out with certain friends.

Frank's passivity came out when he described what had happened during the video game incident.

"I still don't understand what happened at that movie theater," he said. "I don't know how I got pulled into that."

"It's not so hard to understand," the therapist said. "You and two other boys just damaged a machine that was other people's property."

"Yeah, but I don't see how I got trapped into that."

"You're doing a passive number on us here," the therapist countered.

"How's that?"

"Listen to your words. Repeat what you just said."

"I said, 'I don't see how I got trapped.' "

"Right. You say you got trapped. You're the victim. People are doing things to you. But think about it for a minute. Who had the *real* power in that situation?"

"Well, it was just the situation. And the guys I was with."

"Think again. Who really had the power over what you yourself did? Did anybody force you to damage that machine?"

"No."

"So, who had the real power?"

"Probably me."

"Probably?"

"Me. I'm the one who had the power."

In subsequent conversations, Frank acknowledged that he had more control over his own life than he had been willing to admit. Also, his parents began to see ways that they could break through the passive barrier he had erected around himself.

With a passive person, it's very important never to get hooked into answering his questions. Instead, you have to go directly to the underlying assumptions behind those questions.

Teenagers like Frank will always fall back on a victim role, but parents must not allow them to get away with this. Emphasize that they're not pawns or victims in life; they really do have power which they can use to exercise control over their actions. This type of Wild Child, who understands how his passivity distorts his relationships, can often improve his position significantly. He can learn how to make himself more equal with others, to assert his personal power, and to avoid troublesome situations.

THE KID WHO CARES TOO MUCH

The parents of one of the other boys who was involved with Frank in the above video game incident had to confront a different problem. This boy, Hank, had very high standards for himself and cared deeply about being a perfect person and son. Yet, he frequently fell far short of those standards. When that happened, he would become frustrated and "act out" by giving in to the negative impulses that he so desperately wanted to control.

So here's what occurred when Hank found himself in the movie lobby with Frank and his other friend:

He already knew his parents expected a lot of him. Yet, he suspected that they would never be satisfied unless he turned in near-perfect performances in every area of his life. Periodically, of course, he failed to measure up to his own expectations and to those of his parents (or at least those he *assumed* his parents had). In the face of such failures (or perceived failures), Hank in effect threw up his hands and said to himself, "What's the point? I try and try, but I can never measure up. I just don't care anymore!"

In fact, though, he cared *too much*. His acute sense of inadequacy caused him to act out when he was in this state of mind by doing wild, out-of-control things that he would never do under ordinary circumstances.

That's what happened with the video game problem. Hank had just been through a really bad day, with low marks on a test at school and a chewing out by the basketball coach. His parents had also been giving him a bad time about his poor behavior toward his younger sister. Finally, something just snapped inside and he thought, "Who cares?" So he was primed to take out his frustration and feelings of inadequacy on that video machine.

Hank's parents had to help him understand that he wasn't such a bad person after all when he fell short of his standards. "Your mother and I fall short of our standards—regularly!" his father said. "But I guess we don't always tell you when we make our mistakes. You see a fairly consistent, upstanding image that we project to you and other people. But what you *don't* always see are our failures. From now on, we'll have to share more of these with you."

Also, Hank's parents discovered that he was racked by feelings of guilt when he failed, and he carried that guilt around much of the time because he was unable to forgive himself. The more the guilt built up inside him, the worse he felt, until finally he decided to *act* the way he was *feeling*—i.e., as if nothing really mattered very much.

It took some time for Hank to work through this guilt problem. But with the help of his understanding parents, he found that he could gradually let more and more of it go.

"You have the *power* to let that guilt go," his mother said. "It's up to you. Picture that guilt as a dark brown blob inside your chest. It stays there because you *want* it to stay there. But now, picture yourself just reaching down inside yourself, grabbing that blob with both hands, and throwing it outside your body. That's the way you get rid of the guilt. You *choose* not to feel guilty anymore."

Of course, there are times when guilt is appropriate. Hank *should* have felt guilty about tearing up that machine. That was wrong, and "good" guilt signals that we've made a mistake or hurt someone and we have to make amends.

But once you've asked forgiveness and have done what you need to do to set things right, you have to move on with your life. The guilt has to be put aside; that's when it becomes appropriate to reach inside and throw out that brown blob.

In the last analysis, then, Hank had to learn to forgive himself. He ceased to be a Wild Child when his talks with his parents helped him understand more about the importance of turning away from unhealthy, lingering guilt and affirming forgiveness toward himself.

THE EMPTY CHILD

Parents should always look more at what the kid *needs* than at what he does.

The Wild Child who resorts to taking something that belongs to someone else—to stealing—is a child who feels empty inside and needs to be filled up. What will fill up such a child? The best answer: appropriate expressions of love. And that usually means the parent's gift of himself more than gifts of things.

Carla developed a problem with shoplifting and also cheating at school (which was nothing more than stealing the work of her classmates). Her parents and teachers saw her as a Wild Child who was fast moving beyond normal childish problem behavior. But what could be done to rescue her and put her back on the path to more constructive, temperate conduct?

Conversations involving Carla, her parents, and a trained counselor revealed that the girl felt unaccepted and unloved. Her parents both worked, and during many of the days and evenings of her life, she had been under the care of a sitter.

Now that she was a teenager, Carla could take care of herself, but she was still a "latchkey kid," who always came home to an empty apartment. Many times, she remained at home alone until 9:00 or 10:00 P.M. because of her parents' work schedules.

To fill the void created by this lonely existence, Carla spent as much time as she could with various friends, but the other kids weren't always available. So she began to browse through shops in the neighborhood; and when no sales clerk was looking, she would pick up an item and walk out with it. Somehow, this petty theft made her feel more of a whole person, though the feelings of satisfaction were fleeting.

It seems that the act of stealing or cheating gave her an opportunity, however inadequate, to reach out and take a little piece of someone else. Also, getting something for nothing moved her up temporarily into a feeling-good comfort zone (remember our Benephobia Scale).

But stealing and cheating are on the same plane as drugs, alcohol, or any other destructive substitutes for truly good feelings. They may provide a quick rush of satisfaction or happiness, but it soon evaporates, and in the end, the person feels worse than he did at the beginning.

Subsequent therapy helped Carla see the destructive track on which her life was running. Her parents also came to realize that it was up to them to alter their busy schedules and provide more time and love to head off their daughter's temptation to steal. Carla's parents realized that they couldn't just provide her with more expensive presents or other substitutes for their actual presence.

It has taken some effort and discipline on the parents' part. But at least two nights a week and one day on weekends, they have managed to devote regular time to conversations with Carla, family outings to movies, or some other joint activity. Although the final results remain to be seen, this teenager is beginning to seem more satisfied with her life, and her shoplifting problem has disappeared completely.

THE WILD CHILD WHOSE PARENTS
PREFER ABUSE

Ironically, some teenagers become Wild Children because their parents actually prefer the hassles and abuse as a distraction from other things that are going on in their lives. So the parents adopt behavior that encourages the child to lose control.

Paul is a tragic illustration of this sort of teenager. His mother, a single parent, actually bragged that her son was usually "incapable of being tamed." She seemed to like his habit of acting out, mostly because his behavior took her mind off her own problems.

This mother had been through a messy divorce and two unhappy love affairs, and she was constantly beset by anxieties. Her worries included her finances, her lack of prospects for marriage, and her inability to get a promotion at work. Somehow, Paul's problems seemed less significant than her own, and so in a perverse way, she found herself looking forward to his temper tantrums, wild car rides with friends, and general lack of obedience to her.

She once told a friend in Paul's presence, "Even at ten years of age, Paul used to get up from his bed in the middle of the night, go downstairs, get some food, and watch television—even when I told him he couldn't!"

At that, Paul shouted, "I *never* turned on the television set!"

"Wait a minute," the friend said. "I don't understand. What does that mean, when you say you never turned on the set?"

"I *never, ever* turned on that set!" Paul repeated.

"I'm still confused," the friend replied.

"What I mean is, I *did* get up after we went to bed and I *did* get some food. But I listened to the stereo. I *never* turned on the TV!"

"Why is that so important—that you didn't turn on the TV?" the friend asked.

"Because she told us never to turn on that set, and so I didn't."

Somewhere, this mother had communicated that it was absolutely prohibited to turn on the TV, and Paul obeyed. But she laid down few if any other limits on his behavior. Yet, as we've seen in other contexts, all children, including teenagers, have to be given rules and limits. Paul was hungering for guidelines for his life; that's why he focused in a disproportionate way on his mother's TV rule.

Unfortunately, though, this mother chose to allow her son to abuse and disobey her in almost every other area of her life. As a result, the boy's behavior grew worse and worse. Finally, he went on a wild drinking spree one weekend with some friends and got into an auto accident. He was killed instantly—a sad but too-common end for the Wild Child whose parents fail to correct dangerous behavior in time.

THE CHALLENGE OF CONTROL

What's the best way to bring a Wild Child under control? We've already explored some of the possibilities, including helping the teenager to understand himself better; showing more parental love; and setting stricter limits on unruly behavior. Sometimes, however, it's necessary to stop the child in his tracks and correct him on the spot, before his actions become any more destructive.

That brings us to the issue of punishment. As a general rule, I oppose any parental actions that humiliate a child, no matter how bad the child has been. It takes very little for the parent to communicate disapproval to the child. A word or two, a gesture, or a frown is usually all that's required. Parents have all the power in a family situation, and they must learn to use it sparingly, wisely, and incisively. Those who are too free in upbraiding or bullying their children will almost surely provoke a rebellion as the child gets older. And with outright rebellion, there is no reasonable communication, only war.

Also, remember this: What your child wants most is your approval. If he knows you disapprove, you've made your point without rubbing it in.

Spanking or corporal punishment is a form of rubbing in disapproval, and I believe it's unnecessary in disciplining teenagers. Parents should look for other means to get their point across. Of course, I realize that most parents still approve of spanking. A 1988 Harris poll found that 86 percent of adults say it's OK for parents to hit, spank, or physically discipline their children. Also, according to a 1989 Gallup poll, 56 percent of school teachers approve of spankings in school!

But I disagree with these attitudes. In my experience with families and teenagers, I've found that the parents who have to spank are the parents who have failed in some way to get important messages of love and concern across to their children.

So does this mean I'm against all punishment? It depends on how you define punishment. I believe deeply that parents must set limits on their child's behavior. Also, I think that parents have a responsibility, which they exercise too seldom, to tell their children "no" when they've done something wrong. If Paul's mother had just drawn some limits and said "no" a few times, that boy might still be alive today. Usually, the overwhelming power possessed by the parent enables him to correct a child successfully with just a firmly stated limit or a *no*.

But what if a child just won't observe the limits or persists in defying the parent who says "no"? In that case, there has to be a consequence or sanction. Sometimes, a loss of a privilege may be in order if that loss can be tied directly to the offense. You'll recall the example of the Weird Dresser in the previous chapter, who lost his "earring-wearing privileges" because he wore a gold loop instead of a gold post. There, the loss of privilege was linked clearly to the disobedience.

Another possibility favored by many parents and therapists is the concept of the "time out." Time out means taking time out from your normal activity to reflect on your behavior and to have a chance to correct it. As a practical matter, it may also mean taking an enforced rest from the enjoyable, familiar things you usually do.

At our school, we have a permanent time-out place that we call the "farm." Kids with behavior problems go there to work out their difficulties and prepare to become more constructive members of the community. The farm is a very nurturing place, where everything is done for you. Some of the more mature kids are assigned to the farm to talk to those who are on the farm and help them in various ways. In a way, our farm is a *real* farm because we have various animals roaming around there, like chickens, dogs, and goats.

The kids who go to the farm take part in being sent there. They may tell a visitor that they were sent to the farm, but they participate in the choice. They realize they have a problem and need that time out, to get their lives in order.

Overall, then, my concept of a time-out place is not punitive. It's a chance for the teenager to take a breather and reflect on where he's been and where he's going. He knows he's accepted and loved, even as he's putting in his time on the farm. But he also knows that eventually he has to emerge and get on with his life.

How can this apply to a teenager in an ordinary home situation? It may be appropriate for a teenager to go to his room and think his behavior over before he has any more interactions with the family or his peers. But even in the midst of this correction, the parent must show love and be sure to maintain the bonds of trust. Also, it's essential not to humiliate the teenager; young adults can be deeply wounded if they feel an older adult is demeaning them in any way.

The main idea is to help the teenager understand what he's done wrong and how he can improve his behavior. To this end, it may be helpful to have a discussion and negotiate some form of time out, so that the kid will have an opportunity to work out some of his problems on his own.

I realize that these suggestions about sanctions may seem rather vague or even somewhat weak. But remember: Your teenager is *almost* ready to leave home. He's *almost* an adult. If you resort to punishments that would be more appropriate for an elementary school child, you'll force that young person to withdraw; and almost certainly, you'll cut important lines of communication. Your teenager has considerable power to disobey you if he really wants to. So try to avoid those responses that will drive him away; instead, choose the path that will enfold him in your orbit of concern and love.

CHAPTER 11

The Bored Child

Although I applaud the increasing recognition of human rights among various special-interest groups, I have one main fear about these trends—that the bores of the world will begin to demand equal treatment along with everyone else. In one of my most disturbing nightmares, the bores would hold a convention, elect representatives to public office, demand equal TV time—and might even force me to invite them to my private social functions!

While we can laugh about bores up to a point, one thing that is no joke is the teenager who has lost interest and enthusiasm in life. The Bored Child is one of the tragedies of our society, because his lethargy prevents him from becoming motivated to reach his full potential in school, work, and relationships. Boredom is especially destructive to interactions with other people, because the Bored Child lacks the energy and vivacity that are essential to initiating and continuing meaningful conversations. This type of teenager often just doesn't *want* to talk to parents or anyone else.

Boredom is a misunderstood condition because we talk about

it as though it really exists, when in fact, boredom is the *absence* of emotion. When schedules become too heavy, when anger waxes too hot, when confusion predominates in our lives, boredom may set in. Our inner systems shut down so that we want to withdraw. Boredom, then, is a kind of emotional circuit-breaker.

WHAT TRIGGERS BOREDOM IN A TEENAGER?

The Bored Child emerges in a family when one or more of certain boredom-triggering factors are present. These include suppressed anger; a form of overload that may come from an overpacked schedule or excessive fatigue; and a parent-induced inability to become excited.

Factor #1: Anger

If your child is frequently angry at you or anyone else, this anger may come out in the form of boredom. For example, a student may regularly attend a class that involves academic material which is too difficult or confusing for him. His inability to understand what's going on in the course may first make him angry, and then he may claim to be "bored."

Actually, though, the boredom just reflects a mechanism by which the anger has shut down his emotions. He may yawn, his mind may wander, or he may even nod off—classic signs of boredom. But underneath it all, he's still mad as can be at the situation he's in and the teacher who is running the show.

Another variation of this scenario involved Ann, a seventeen-year-old who had been begging her parents for a telephone for her room. Many of her friends had their own phones, and she felt she deserved this privilege as well.

But her parents saw the situation differently. They felt the extra phone line would be too expensive for their household budget, and they also worried that Ann would waste too much time talking to her friends, rather than concentrating on her schoolwork.

Several arguments occurred over this issue, until finally, the father put his foot down: "You're *not* going to get a phone, so I don't want to hear any more about it!"

With that, the conflict over the phone died down, but simultaneously, Ann's boredom set in. She moped around her room, not really sulking but saying things like, "This house is getting me down. I don't know what to do. There's nobody to go out with."

When her mother suggested some alternatives, such as homework or extra work on one of her extracurricular activities, Ann responded, "I don't feel like that right now. I'm really bored."

In fact, she was *angry*, but the anger had shut down her emotions so that she couldn't get interested in anything. She had become a Bored Child.

To resolve this problem, Ann's parents didn't deal directly with the phone issue and her anger about it. They suspected, quite correctly, that resurrecting this topic would just cause more angry outbursts. Instead, they did two things:

First, they began to inject more humor into their family conversations, such as sharing funny incidents that had happened to them or relating light stories. Just the act of smiling or chuckling a little helped improve Ann's mood and infused her with more personal energy and interest in life.

Next, her parents took more of an initiative in suggesting and promoting activities that increased her enthusiasm. Knowing that homework seemed too much like *real* work and was a poor substitute for the phone she had wanted, Ann's mother began to point the girl toward a school election which interested her. Together, they began to gather campaign materials and brainstorm about vote-getting strategies. Before long, Ann was happily spending her spare time working on school politics, and the phone issue was a thing of the past.

To sum up, then, anger may indeed lead to boredom and a shutdown both of the teenager's emotional resources and of her ability to talk with her parents. But when parents help the youngster to leave the anger behind, the boredom quickly dissipates.

Factor #2: Overload

In our present-day society, many teenagers tend to be overscheduled. They get involved in too many activities, too many teams, too many personal-improvement classes, all on top of their regular homework assignments. Those who are conscientious about fulfilling their obligations and meeting deadlines may respond like many overscheduled adults: Their "interest-in-life systems" begin to shut down. If you don't have the time or energy to handle all you're supposed to do, it's natural to react by saying, "I don't want to do this stuff anymore. It's not interesting."

This form of overload-boredom is often accompanied by a general malaise about interacting productively with other family members. There's a tendency for the weighed-down teenager to become preoccupied with all he hasn't done. In that state of mind, it's hard to concentrate on the conversation of others or to become interested in what they are saying.

Sometimes, the emotional shutdown is selective. Those young people with too much to do may just push off certain responsibilities, such as classwork that is particularly difficult, on the ground that "it's boring." Actually, though, the academic material may not be boring to the child at all *if* he has time to wrestle with it and master it.

Take Seth, a bright fifteen-year-old who usually did quite

well in all his academic subjects. But he had recently become excessively involved in the school's chess and debating teams, and participating in tournaments and other competitions had begun to take their toll on his regular schoolwork. He started complaining about the difficulty of his math course and what he perceived as the inadequacy of his teacher. But his father sensed something wasn't quite on target about these complaints.

"Just a couple of months ago, you told me you liked this course and teacher," the father noted.

"I know, but that's changed."

"How's that?"

"I don't know. The class isn't very interesting anymore. And the teacher is a bore. He doesn't know how to teach."

It was evident that Seth didn't want to talk about this topic any more, and his father let it rest for a day. But then Dad brought the subject up again and probed until he learned that the main problem was that Seth didn't have time to think through his homework assignments.

"I guess I might like math this year if that's all I had to do, or at least if I could put in more time on it. In fact, just the other day, I did spend some extra time working on one problem. That was a lot of fun, finding a solution that most of the other students didn't get."

Seth became animated as he described his success with that assignment, but before long, he lapsed back into his bored look again. It was apparent that the problem wasn't with the course or the teacher, but with Seth's overloaded schedule. When he took the time to think through his homework assignments and work hard on them, he really liked them. On the other hand, when he didn't or couldn't make the time, he became frustrated, then a little angry, and finally, bored.

To resolve the problem, Seth's father suggested simply that

perhaps the boy should eliminate some of the things from his busy schedule. That way, he would have more time to devote to his homework *and* more time to enjoy it.

Seth quickly saw the wisdom of this advice and decided to quit the chess club. He knew he was better at debating than chess, and dropping out of this activity wouldn't cause him much disappointment. The opening in his schedule freed Seth to devote more time to fewer responsibilities, with the result that he became more excited about his homework and debating, and decidedly less bored.

Becoming overloaded is a complex subject, because this tendency may lead to burnout, high anxiety, or other states that have nothing to do with boredom. But sometimes, boredom, in the form of a shut-down of all emotions, may be the end result. Excessive frustration, anger, and confusion may arise from a too-heavy schedule, and the child finds that he just can't handle it.

Furthermore, the preoccupation and inner deadness that accompanies this response to pressure can be extremely destructive to family communication. Yet, more often than not, the solution to the problem may be quite simple: namely, just cutting back on the extra activities and responsibilities that are causing the problem.

Factor #3: An Inability to Become Excited

Some teenagers seem chronically unable to become excited about anything. They always appear to be bored. I'm reminded of a sixteen-year-old girl, Effie, who always looked as though she was about to drop off to sleep. In fact, those who tried to engage in a conversation with her often would begin to feel sleepy, too!

It wasn't that this girl was unusually shy or a poor conversationalist. She really *was* bored with life, and that made her a boring person. She seemed incapable of getting excited about anything. As a result, it was difficult for anyone to engage her in a good conversation about anything.

What about her parents? How did they relate to her?

They were a large part of the problem. They *also* were bored and boring people, they consistently resisted showing or feeling excitement. A typical conversation between Effie and her mother:

Effie: "I got my grade back on that big English test."

Mom: "Oh, how did you do?"

Effie: "I got an A."

Mom: "Oh, that's nice. So what are you going to do this afternoon?"

No emotional response here. No sense of excitement or pride. No words of affirmation that might suggest, "Hey, that's great, Effie—you're really doing well!"

Predictably, Effie's lack of excitement about life, including her general air of boredom and unconcern, could be traced to what she had learned from her parents. Both emphasized that it was best not to talk about yourself or your accomplishments too much, because that might be interpreted as boasting or self-centeredness.

Effie learned her lessons well. When parents are bored or boring, children may also become bored or boring. The emotional trait—or in this case, *lack* of emotion—will be communicated to the child as the norm for feeling and conduct.

I remember Effie primarily as a child who sighed a lot; who played down her accomplishments and those of others; and who generally tended to be isolated from her peers. Also, her ability to talk with her parents was severely limited because of the cap they had placed on any expression of exuberant, joyful feelings.

Unfortunately, resolving a situation like this successfully depends on the parents' being willing to introduce more excitement and *non*boring feelings and expressions into their lives and conversations. They weren't able to do this, and so the family continued to reinforce the boredom that was imposing such limits on Effie's emotional potential. In such cases, then, parents must be willing to become better role models and thereby, through their own example, to *teach* excitement to their kids. By this means, they will be in a better position to break through the boredom that is erecting barriers to communication.

POSITIVE SUBSTITUTES FOR BOREDOM

It's important for parents to find antidotes to the boredom their children feel, both to promote more energy and excitement in the teenager *and* to head off destructive reactions the kids may come up with themselves.

Although some passive people may become resigned to a certain level of boredom in their lives, no one *likes* to feel bored. Bored people know they are living below their comfort zone on the Benephobia Scale. So the most natural impulse for the Bored Child is to take some action that will help him shake off his boredom and begin to feel happier and more enthusiastic. The most constructive function parents can perform is to guide the teenager toward the most desirable solution to his boredom.

So more specifically, what can parents do to help their teenagers get more involved and interested in life?

One approach that has worked well for us at our school is to emphasize *positive substitutes* for boredom, as well as for more active negative experiences like drugs, alcohol use, or promiscuous sex. For example, we try to arrange regular trips to exciting places like Russia or Mexico for dozens of kids who may be performing in a play or concert. These adventures provide exhilarating, abiding thrills that go far beyond the temporary highs that drugs can offer. Just as important, from the kids' point of view they're far preferable to a constant state of boredom!

Parents might try the same thing on a less global scale by arranging interesting weekend trips, day adventures, or creative parties for their teenagers. Obviously, when you're dealing with an adolescent who is on the verge of adulthood, you can't set up "play dates" as you would for a preschooler. Many times, the teenager doesn't want his parents around at social functions. Also, he'll typically demand a considerable degree of independence in making decisions about how to use his time.

But with the Bored Child, the parent will usually have to take more of an initiative than with other types of teenagers. The Bored Child is, by definition, locked in a passive state of personal vegetation. So Mom or Dad will often need to make suggestions or make some initial plans and arrangements to get things moving.

Some possibilities I've encountered in different families:

- Once a month, plan a family outing that everyone, and especially the teenager, really likes. Some families love to hike, camp, or play tennis together; others like cultural events like concerts; still others prefer to go to professional athletic contests.

    If possible, the outing should be an unusual treat, something the teenager normally wouldn't do alone. That way, it will be harder for him to turn it down. Events such as these serve two functions: a forum to allow all members of the family to communicate at length with one another; and an exciting inspiration that will encourage the Bored Child to break free of his ennui.

- Buy tickets to a special event, such as a rock concert,

and give them to your teenager so that she can take a friend or two to the function.

• Turn your home over to your child at least one evening a month, so that he can have a small party with his peers.

• Take the family to a local church or synagogue that has an all-family program, including well-organized teenage groups and activities. A few trips to church can introduce a teenager to an entirely new set of friends and quickly eliminate any boredom.

These are simple, obvious suggestions, but it's amazing to me how many parents fail to understand how much fun and interest they can bring into a bored teenager's life. More often than not, the mother or father will bemoan the fact that the child is moping about the house. But they don't try the easy solutions that are nearest at hand to remedy the problem.

THE SUPER-HERO SOLUTION

Finally, one of the most exciting *and* controversial ideas for beating boredom and a host of other ills—including those which afflict many Wild Children and other Kid Types—is what might be called the "Super-Hero Solution." I mention this approach not to suggest that it's right for every family or child, because it's not. In fact, used the wrong way, this sort of behavior may be downright dangerous. But I think you'll agree that the creativity involved here can at least serve as an inspiration for those trying to introduce more constructive excitement into teenagers' lives.

The first instance I encountered of the Super-Hero Solution involved a kid who had been in a lot of trouble with the police.

He used to break into houses and steal things and had also used drugs and alcohol. Then, someone introduced him to karate, and he quickly became enamored of the sport and moved on to get a black belt.

But when he had mastered the martial arts, he found he was getting restless again. In short, for a time he lapsed into the Bored Child syndrome. Remembering the old patterns of conduct, his parents feared that to relieve the emptiness he might resort once more to crime and drugs. But then, inexplicably, he turned into a very happy kid, very outgoing and interested in school and classmates. His parents couldn't figure it out and neither could I—until finally, during one of our classes, he disclosed what he had been up to and the reason for his satisfaction.

It seems that he had always harbored fantasies about being a super-hero like Batman, Spider Man, or Superman. So with his newly acquired karate skills, he decided to *become* a super-hero! A couple of nights a week, he donned a black karate outfit, slipped out of the house, and roamed the streets, looking for innocent victims to defend. On more than one occasion, he intervened in muggings or harassment incidents and sent the offenders running away with a kick or two.

Dangerous business, to be sure! But when this boy told his story, four other kids confessed that they had entertained the same fantasy and done similar things on occasion!

Now, I don't advocate that parents encourage their children to try something quite this daring, and I would strongly discourage any of my students from engaging in such shenanigans. But the basic idea isn't so bad. The trick is to find a way to become a super-hero without turning into a vigilante or law-enforcement problem.

A safer alternative to the Super-Hero Solution was employed by a girl who did "sneaky" good deeds that no one would know she had done. For example, she would bake some cookies or buy some flowers and take them over to an elderly shut-in who lived nearby. The teenager would attach a note that might say, "From a secret admirer" or, "For all the great things you've done for others."

That's the best, most realistic way for a teenager to be a super-hero. And those who find equally creative, exciting ways to serve others will find they have little time or inclination to be bored.

CHAPTER 12

The Clam

The type of kid that I call the Clam is common in many households. In fact, most kids seem to go through a Clam phase at one time or another. What are the signs that you may have a Clam living with you?

- He may be unusually secretive.
- She may lock her door frequently, or lock one or more drawers in her room.
- He may refuse to talk about some—or many—aspects of his life.

This tendency to become secretive or to "clam up" is common among teenagers for a number of reasons, some of which are a normal part of growing up, and some of which may be cause for serious parental concern.

WHY KIDS CLAM UP

I've run into many different species of Clam, though in most cases they can reduced to five main categories: the newly independent; the natural loner; the drug abuser; the sexually active; and the denier.

The Newly Independent Clam

Parents are often disappointed and may be shocked or angered when their clingy, loving, preadolescent child experiences the onset of puberty. With the hormonal and growth changes that occur during sexual maturation, emotional transformations also occur—notably, the drive of the child to separate from his mother and father and assert his independence.

This natural development of separation is nothing to worry about. In fact, it's something for parents to celebrate, because the desire of the child to leave behind his dependence on Mom and Dad is a healthy sign, an indication that early family nurture and preparation has succeeded.

Still, difficulties in communicating with adolescents can be frustrating, especially for parents who have grown accustomed to closeness and sharing with the child in earlier years. How can you establish a good talking relationship with this type of teenager? More on this in the section below on how to get a Clam to open up. But first, let's explore some other types of Clam behavior.

The Natural Loner Clam

Every child needs affection, intimacy, and in-depth communication from her parents—but not all kids need this contact in the same amounts or doses. Some are naturally very affectionate, open, and talkative; others are more reserved, distant, or stand-offish.

I'm reminded of one boy who tended to "keep his own counsel" from the early elementary school years. He never told his parents what was happening at school; never asked for help on his homework; and rarely shared his feelings about himself or his classmates.

The same "loner" traits continued up into adolescence. This boy almost never disclosed to his parents what he was thinking, and almost always made his own decisions, without advance parental consultation.

These characteristics worried his mother and father at first, because they feared the boy needed more adult guidance. They were concerned that he might make foolish choices and maybe even succumb to peer pressures and get involved in problem behavior, such as drug abuse. But in fact, his independence was a deep-rooted trait that had been a part of his personality from the beginning. As it turned out, his inclination to operate on his own gave him more confidence than many of his classmates and placed him in a leadership position in many activities as he got older.

For some children, then, the failure to communicate a great deal with parents and other adults may simply be a natural attribute that doesn't signal any major communications problem. In some cases, the trait may actually work to the teenager's advantage. On the other hand, other kinds of Clams may present more worries for Mom and Dad.

The Drug Abuser Clam

Nick, a fifteen-year-old boy, had moved steadily into the use and abuse of alcohol and drugs, beginning at about age thirteen. He and his parents had never been able to talk freely about their feelings, and the family's instruction in values had been defective.

The mother and father occasionally said things like, "We

hope you're staying away from drugs and booze at these parties you're attending." But they frequently came in from social gatherings tipsy themselves, and Nick knew from adult conversations he had overheard that they dabbled in cocaine and marijuana. So regardless of what these parents *said*, the message they communicated through their actions was, "Drugs and alcohol are OK."

Like many substance abusers, Nick maintained a secret side to his life: He locked his door frequently and always kept at least one drawer in his room locked. When his mother questioned him about this practice, he glowered and replied curtly, "It's my room, and I need privacy!"

She didn't question him further because she assumed that his secrecy was just part of growing up and becoming independent. But something bothered these parents about the clandestine side of their boy, especially when he came home on weekends looking glassy-eyed or with a whiff of alcohol on his breath.

He always explained the alcohol away by saying, "I just had a taste of punch at the party—I didn't know it was spiked." As for the reddened or glassy eyes, he said, "I didn't get much sleep last night." Or, "The room I was in had a lot of smoke."

Then, Nick went away for several weeks to be a camp counselor during the summer, and he called to request that his parents send a package to him that he kept in his locked desk drawer. After telling his father where the key was, he warned, "This package is a private thing of mine. I don't want anyone to look in it, OK?"

But his father had finally had enough. He immediately got the key, opened the drawer, tore open the package—and found an assortment of pills, cocaine, and marijuana.

Nick obviously knew there was something wrong with what he was keeping in that drawer. That was why he kept it locked and behaved so secretively. At the same time, he seemed to be reaching out for some advice, and the only way he knew how to begin a dialogue with his parents was to set himself up to be discovered. Down deep, he wanted that cloak of secrecy to be lifted so that he could deal more effectively with his problem, and fortunately, his father responded appropriately.

There were some accusations that flew back and forth at first. But when tempers cooled off, both the mother and father acknowledged that they had been bad examples and that they would try to do better. As you might imagine, to change the ingrained, longstanding negative behavior in this family wasn't a very easy order, and both the parents and the teenager are still trying to work through the difficult issues of alcohol and drug abuse. But at least the issues are on the table, where everyone can see them and confront them openly.

The Sexually Active Clam

Marisa began smoking when she was fourteen, and at about the same time, she began to have sex with her boyfriend. When they broke up, she immediately entered into a sexual liaison with another boy; then, that arrangement ended and another one began.

Typically, Marisa would demand the key to her father's den downstairs for her dates, or she would just take her date up to her bedroom when her parents were out of the house. She never told her mother and father what she was doing, but from the voices and sounds that came through the door at times, the activity was obvious. The issue finally came to a head when the parents came home one evening and found Marisa in the *parents'* bed with a new boyfriend.

This mother and father began to see a counselor because they were understandably worried about sexually transmitted diseases and other potential problems with their daughter's behavior.

"But I don't want to inhibit her sexually," her father said. "I grew up in an extremely repressed sexual environment, and I don't want to expose her to that. Besides, I don't think there's anything wrong with her having some sex. I just think there have to be some ground rules around the house."

As the discussions with the therapist progressed, it became evident to both parents that they were afraid to confront Marisa because they knew their own moral beliefs and values were on shaky ground. Even though the father gave lip service to an open attitude toward his daughter's sex life, on a deeper level he felt extremely uncomfortable with her behavior. As for the mother, she thought this level of sex before marriage was wrong, but she was unclear in her own mind where the lines should be drawn.

The answer in this case? There really has been no answer up to this point except that the counselor has encouraged the parents to open up more lines of communication with their daughter. Her free sexual activity—and especially her most recent caper of hopping into her parents' bed with a boyfriend—suggests an attempt to *escalate* outrageous behavior in order to get her parents' attention. She really wants information; she wants guidance; she wants to talk.

Finally, her parents are responding, and together, they are all working out a sexual ethic that at least has a chance of being more reasonable and workable than their current one. In this case, as in many others, it all began with opening a conversation; then, once the parents and child were talking, they used their natural imagination and creativity to formulate together some solutions and action plans.

The Denyer Clam

Some teenage Clams may not be primarily secretive; instead, their main thing is that they *deny* that they have a problem. In their denial, they turn a deaf ear to their parents and others who might help them. In the final analysis, they refuse to discuss important issues.

One girl, whom I dubbed "Cleopatra, the Queen of Denial," would turn me off like a human TV set when I wanted to engage her in important issues that I knew were disturbing her. Her grades had deteriorated, and several friendships had fallen apart, mainly because of a preoccupation she had with problems at home.

I knew she worried constantly about her mother, who had been sent to a mental rehabilitation facility, and about her parents' marriage, which seemed about to end. Yet, I had to guess at the specifics or pick them up from other sources, because this young woman simply wouldn't talk about them.

"Cleopatra" had erected a shield around herself—a shield of denial—which carried the message, "Don't mess with me. I'm not interested in talking about personal issues."

This sort of denial of a problem occurs because the person assumes, often subconsciously, that if she doesn't talk about the problem, maybe she'll stop thinking about it. And if she stops thinking about it, maybe it will go away. Of course, she *didn't* stop thinking about her family's difficulties, and they *didn't* go away.

Gently, but persistently, I kept the pressure on her because I knew the only way that inner healing could occur was for her to get rid of that protective outer cloak.

"How are you doing today?" I'd ask.

"Fine. Just fine."

"Really? I don't believe you. I just saw you arguing with Joan."

"It's a private thing."

"Is it? Well, Joan seems to be involved."

"Michael, I really don't think I want to talk about it."

"It's up to you. But I'm here when you need me, OK? And remember: Dealing with some of the things inside yourself can begin with an open talk."

Finally, this young Clam fell apart emotionally, as many serious denyers do. The pressures at home, at school, and among her friends were too onerous. She couldn't maintain that shell she had tried to build to ward off the stresses and strains of her life. So the shell cracked, and the emotions poured forth—and that was a good thing. As she finally began to talk to me, her surrogate parent, all that frustration, anger, and pain she had been trying to hold inside came out along with the tears and complaints.

With the Denyer Clam, parents must keep probing in an effort to break through the shell. The tapping and knocking on the outer shield has to be done carefully but courageously. You have to sense when to stop; but don't be afraid to push a little. There's a fine line between wise parental assertiveness and nagging. But with a denyer, more constructive things are likely to be accomplished by going a little too far than by not going far enough.

HOW TO GET A CLAM TO OPEN UP

So far, you've been introduced to a number of different types of Clams, and you've seen how breakthroughs have been achieved with a few. But more needs to be said about ways to open up a Clam. To this end, I'd suggest you consider some "opening-up" principles that have worked many times for me.

Principle #1: Make Yourself Vulnerable

The first rule of getting a Clam—or any child, for that matter—to open up is that you, the parent, must first demonstrate openness. That means you have to put yourself on the line, make yourself vulnerable by confessing something you've done wrong, or admitting some doubt or uncertainty about your own life or conduct.

When the teenager sees a pattern developing where his parents are consistently opening up, then he'll gain confidence that he's living in an open environment which allows *him* to open up safely as well.

Our community at the DeSisto School strives to establish an open and vulnerable atmosphere for a couple of reasons. First of all, we've found that it requires a lot more energy to hold in feelings and emotions—to be *un*open—than it does just to talk freely about things.

Second, kids are almost always more scared of adults than adults are of kids; so parents are usually in a stronger position to get things started than their children. Your child may worry, "If I tell Dad about this, he's really going to lay into me. He's going to take away all my privileges!" Unless they somehow learn otherwise, teenagers aren't naturally going to expose themselves to penalties. But they *can* learn otherwise if you take the first step in becoming vulnerable.

Principle #2: Push at the Child's Pace

I'm not sure there's anything worse in family communication for a parent to tell a kid, "Talk to me!"

The way you get a teenager to talk is for *you* the *parent* to talk and share, *not* to insist that the youngster carry the ball first. In one family, the father could almost always count on starting an argument, or causing his teenage son to "close down" or clam up, by asking, "So what happened in school today?"

Invariably, the boy would feel the parent was prying, and so he would sidestep the question. This would make the father alternately curious and irritated, until many times he would end with, "Well, I don't see why you're shutting your family out of your life, but that's your business!"

In such situations, I often suggest that the parent put himself in the teenager's shoes. Then, I asked, "How would you like it if you were constantly bombarded with questions about work when you didn't feel like talking?" If something nice or exciting or disturbing happened to you and you want to share it, it's likely that you'll be the one to initiate the conversation.

It's the same with your child. To engage him in a scintillating discussion, you have to go at his pace and talk about those things *he* wants to share. Anything else may range from a boring interchange, to unpleasant parental pushiness, to verbal rape.

It's the same with physical contact. Affectionate hugs, pats, and kisses all have their place in the parent-child relationship. In fact, I believe that some physical contact is essential to enable a child to grow up with a feeling of being secure and loved. But it's deadly to parent-child interaction if the mother or father is always pushing himself physically on the child.

You have probably already noticed that a gradual physical disengagement is occurring between you and your kids, a separation that proceeds steadily in the continuum between childhood and adolescence. For example, life may be full of hugs, kisses, and hand-holding between a father and son up to about age four or five. Then, the son will want to pick his special times and places for the hugs and kisses; at other times, he wants to be unrestrained, on the move, up and about at play and other interests.

The handholding may continue fairly freely up to about age ten, eleven, or even twelve. At that point, however, the boy is likely to want to *let go* of Dad's hand when other boys his age are nearby. The reason? That growing need to be more separate and independent.

Finally, the handholding will cease entirely, but the hugging may continue, so long it's done at the child's time and place. The operative concept here is *go at your child's pace*.

That way, you can be more certain that you're promoting the most conducive environment for real communication with your teenager.

Principle #3: Get a Kick out of Conflict

One of the best ways to open up a Clam is to start a friendly argument. You may protest, "We already have too many fights in our family!" But I'm not talking about fighting; I'm referring to a civilized, joking dispute which should end in laughs and excitement, rather than hard feelings.

One father-daughter combination had tremendous fun arguing about which musical instrument was better, guitar or violin. As it happened, the father played the guitar, and the thirteen-year-old girl played violin.

"You can play more singable songs with a guitar," the father said.

"You can play more popular *and* classical music on a violin," the daughter countered.

"That's only true if you could play the violin as well as I play the guitar."

"Oh, come on, Daddy!"

Finally, the bantering ended in a challenge of skills, which resulted in a jam session in the living room. All kids like a challenge, especially if they think there's a good chance that they will come out ahead of a parent. A sense of challenge leads to enhanced interest, which in turn leads to more honest conversations and sharing.

Caution: Obviously, this approach can be taken too far. The parent who decides to push beyond the bounds of fun in an effort to "win" a friendly argument will inevitably lose in the relationship. So try to get a kick out of your little conflicts *without* provoking or exasperating your youngsters.

Principle #4: Talk About Your Teenager in the Third Person

This "third-person technique" may seem a strange piece of advice, but I've found it to be an effective and playful little trick for getting a Clam to open up. Here's how this approach worked with Sybil and her parents.

Sybil was a shy, reserved twelve-year-old who had no particular problems except that she didn't enter easily into sensitive discussions about her thoughts or feelings. Her parents had tried the direct route—"Tell us about your feelings" or, "Tell us about what happened in school today"—but those attempts had fallen flat.

Then, they began to use the third-person technique, which went like this:

Dad to Mom: "You know, I think Sybil is trying to put something over on me."

Mom to Dad: "What do you mean?"

Dad to Mom: "She's trying to trick me into driving her and Cathy to a movie tomorrow."

By this time, Sybil is all ears, and she's smiling.

Mom to Dad: "Now, I don't think Sybil would try to trick anybody."

Dad to Mom: "Oh yeah? Well, she tries to trick me all the time—and besides, I don't think that movie is too good for a couple of young women."

Sybil: "Come on, Daddy! You know there's nothing wrong with that movie!"

From here, the conversation might go in any number of interesting and fun directions. But the point is that Sybil has become engaged in the conversation. Furthermore, with the ongoing protection and distraction of humor, she's more likely to interact openly in the future with her parents.

174 DECODING YOUR TEENAGER

* * *

There are many ways to get a Clam to open up, just as there are many types of Clams. As I said at the beginning of this chapter, most teenagers I've known go through this phase at some point as a natural part of growing up. It's up to the parent to determine what kind of Clam behavior is normal, and what kind may signal more serious underlying problems—and then to respond accordingly.

CHAPTER 13

The Insecure Child

For a variety of reasons—which often are hidden in a peculiar configuration of genes or obscured by the erased memories of early childhood—a sense of insecurity may arise in teenagers. There are several signs that you may be involved with an Insecure Child:

- He may be a classic overachiever.
- She may be weighed down by guilt and seem unable to accept forgiveness or love herself.
- He may constantly be looking for approval from others.
- She may demonstrate a marked lack of self-confidence.

What is the impact of such insecurity on the teenager's ability to communicate with parents? The main problem is that this type of young person tends to focus mostly on his personal inadequacies and his need to gain the approval of others. In such a state, he can't interact from a position of strength with another person.

He becomes incapable of talking and communicating as a valuable individual in his own right.

To understand how this dynamic can work, let's take a closer look at two different variations of the Insecure Child—the overachiever and the guilt-ridden youngster.

THE CLASSIC OVERACHIEVER

Often, we applaud and hold up as models those teenagers who excel at their academic work, rise to the top in extracurricular activities, or in general turn in performances that outstrip those of their peers. But there may be more to high achievement than meets the eye.

Sometimes, the teenager who is very good in one or several fields is driven by a profound sense of insecurity. Greg, a seventeen-year-old student-body president and star athlete, was ranked at the top of his class when he applied to college, and he was admitted to one of the nation's top institutions. But he seemed increasingly unable to *enjoy* his accomplishments. Furthermore, he couldn't seem to relax and just chat with others unless the conversation was goal-oriented.

His friends had noticed the intensity in Greg's personality first and had accused him jokingly of being overly ambitious or too much of a "teenage workaholic." Greg's parents, on hearing about these comments, first wrote them off as jealousy. But then they also began to pick up tendencies Greg had to focus almost exclusively on his *objectives* in sports, in school politics, or in his courses. He seemed to have little interest in the activities or needs of other people or family members.

Initially, Greg's mother and father wondered if perhaps their son was simply becoming selfish or egocentric. But certain telltale signs suggested to them that there was more to the problem

than this. In particular, they were alerted to an increasing inci-
dence of some rather peculiar comments and questions from Greg,
such as:

"I may have made it into my first-pick college, but I've got to
be careful. One slip, and they might decide they don't want me."

Or, "Dad, I made the *Who's Who* listing for American high
school students—I guess that means I'm really somebody!"

Or, "I'm not sure I really like all these things I'm doing. It's
important for me to reach the top and be the best, but after I do
that, I can't seem to stop and *enjoy* what's I've achieved. I have
this restless feeling that it's time to move on to the next thing."

These and similar statements indicated that Greg suffered
from a profound lack of confidence in himself, despite his tremendous achievements. In discussions with a family religious
counselor, he revealed that he felt he had to *do* things and *accomplish* goals in order to be accepted as a good person.

By whom did he want so desperately to be accepted? That
wasn't entirely clear. He wasn't conscious of feeling that he had
to please anyone. When pushed, however, he acknowledged that
he was probably working mainly to be accepted by his parents
and other adult authority figures, such as his coaches and teachers.

Further counseling sessions confirmed that Greg was incapable of feeling good about himself and his achievements. He
withheld praise from himself because he feared, as he said at one
point, "If I let myself feel good about what I've done, then
maybe I'll stop feeling or being successful." And without constant, recurrent success in his life, he would be in danger of not
being accepted by the people who mattered most, especially his
mother and father.

In effect, Greg had become shackled onto a treadmill of
achievement. Instead of working hard because he enjoyed what
he was doing or because his activities and studies were meaningful

in themselves, he labored only to get the plaudits and approval of others. Ironically, though, his parents didn't appear to care as much about his achievements as Greg did.

"Sure, we're proud of him and we're happy he's going to a fine college, but there's more to life than that," his father told the counselor. "Neither his mother nor I did as much at such a young age as he has, and we're both a little worried that he's going to burn himself out."

There was no overt indication of pushiness on the part of these parents. So where did Greg's excessive urge to achieve come from?

The sources of his inner drive never became entirely clear in counseling, and those who knew him well could only speculate. One possibility was that he was just born with an ambitious, achievement-prone personality.

Another thought is that somehow, he had come to feel a subtle lack of acceptance on the part of his parents. A closer examination of the family pattern revealed that Greg, the eldest of four children, had been placed in highly competitive situations beginning when he was quite young. For example:

- He had played on Little League and soccer teams from age six.
- He had taken language lessons and other extracurricular courses from his kindergarten years.
- He had been strongly encouraged to "take advantage of every opportunity," such as running for various school offices and otherwise assuming leadership roles.

When he did well in these activities, both his parents made it a point to praise him lavishly. When he didn't do so well, he received less attention. In fact, coming from a relatively large family, he found that the best way to attract the positive attention of his busy parents was to achieve. Probably, this desire to please or be noticed by his parents combined with natural talents, energy, and ambition to produce an insecure overachiever.

Now that Greg and his parents are more aware of the problem, he is taking steps to build more unstructured "down time" into his busy schedule. Like most overachievers, Greg knows that to continue to reach his goals and do well at his chosen activities, he needs the good will of those around him. Among other things, that means being able to talk with friends and coworkers, as well as family members. His emotional maturity has enabled him to take significant steps to overcome his feelings of insecurity and to achieve without undercutting his important relationships.

INSECURE THOUGH INNOCENT!

Many children go through a guilt-obsessed stage when they are very young, but by the time they reach adolescence, the guilt is usually expressed more appropriately. For instance, one eight-year-old girl kept asking her parents, "Do you forgive me? Do you forgive me?" after small infractions. They would assure her, "Of course we forgive you!" But still, she would chime in with that litany, "Are you *sure* you forgive me?"

Such behavior is usually nothing to worry about in such a young child, and in a short time, this particular girl did move beyond this phase in her development. But if a teenager continues to respond this way after small or nonexistent transgressions, he may be subject to excessive feelings of guilt. Such a child probably has deep-seated insecurities which have to be resolved so that he can learn to forgive himself and get on with his life.

Sue, an extremely caring fifteen-year-old, had a reputation

for being one of the kindest and most altruistic people in her class. But it became something of a joke among her peers that "if you want someone to blame, check with Sue—she'll confess to anything."

In short, Sue was a person who automatically assumed that she was in the wrong and others were in the right when accusations started to fly about. If someone became angry or otherwise disagreed with her, Sue always looked to herself first and never imagined that the fault might lie elsewhere.

Of course, most people are the opposite. When the average person comes under attack, the natural tendency is to become defensive and to point the finger of blame elsewhere. But Sue focused on her own inadequacies and shortcomings, even when it was difficult or impossible to identify exactly what they were.

The source for this attitude could be traced to Sue's relationship with her mother, who constantly made her feel guilty and inadequate. From an early age, Mom would bombard her with criticisms:

"You didn't make your bed right."

"You didn't pick up all your clothes."

"You don't really love me, do you?"

"Don't you have any concern at all for your parents?"

"A child who really appreciated her mother wouldn't do that."

These comments sank in, and Sue soon came to believe that she was always inadequate and guilty. Also, she sensed she wouldn't be worthy of her mother's love unless she pleased her by serving her in various ways. But of course, nothing that Sue ever did was enough. Her mother always found something to criticize and some means to deepen her daughter's feelings of guilt.

Such distortions in the parent-child relationship can be quite damaging to free, open, and life-changing conversation. There's no way that a mother or father can be a good adviser to a teenager or serve as a constructive influence in the transition to adulthood when excessive guilt is getting in the way. In my opinion, playing on a child's guilty feelings is actually a form of emotional child abuse.

Also, the parent inevitably hurts herself as well as her child by playing on guilt. For one thing, the adult who engenders guilt in a young person will herself become overly dependent and may experience stunted emotional development. Also, a parent can't develop a satisfying peer relationship with a son or daughter later in life unless guilt is put into proper perspective.

To deal more effectively with this type of guilty kid, I have suggested that Sue, her mother, and people like them consider these three "Guidelines for Guilt."

Guideline #1: Distinguish Between Healthy and Unhealthy Guilt

I'm not in favor of throwing out all feelings of guilt because healthy guilt—that is, guilt that arises from true wrongdoing—is a powerful corrective to those who break the laws and values of civilized society. If a child verbally abuses a parent, for instance, it's appropriate for the child to feel guilty, apologize, and try to set the relationship straight again.

On the other hand, it may be quite right for a child to disagree or take an opposing stand when a parent engages in some moral inconsistency or other aberrant behavior. Sue in the above illustration hadn't learned how to distinguish between unhealthy guilt, which she seemed to feel all the time, and healthy guilt.

Remember one of our basic principles about parent-child relationships: Parents have job descriptions and so do their kids. One of the kids' functions is to be the "moral security agent" of the family, and so long as that role is fulfilled respectfully, there should be nothing to feel guilty about.

Guideline #2: Learn to Forgive Yourself

Sue in the above example always thought she was in the wrong because, in the first instance, she had not learned to forgive herself. She held on to real and imagined guilt so that she actually *lived* in an *environment* of guilt!

The first step in her dealing with this problem was simply to let go of the guilt—let it flow through her, but then right out of her life again. It helps if you have someone in authority to say, "There's no need for you to feel guilty about this or that," but unfortunately, her mother couldn't manage this role. So Sue began meeting with her local pastor who provided sufficient authority to help her believe, "You really *are* forgiven—by God and by me!"

This reinforcement helped her accept that she truly had forgiveness. So it became easier to let go of the guilt she was harboring.

Guideline #3: Distinguish Between Being Selfish and Self-loving

Too often, overly guilty teenagers and adults fall into the trap of thinking that loving yourself is the same as being selfish. Any good feelings these teens have toward themselves somehow seem wrong, and with that misdirected sense of wrong comes guilt.

But in fact, it's *right* to love ourselves, and a balanced interpretation of most religious philosophies would support this point of view. For example, when Jesus says that the second greatest commandment is "You shall love your neighbor as yourself," there's an assumption that his hearers *do* love themselves.

When your guilty teenager can truly accept the fact that she is worth loving and that it's OK for her to love herself, she'll be well on the road to overcoming her insecurities. Just as important, she'll be in a position to participate and grow emotionally as a full member of family discussions.

CHAPTER 14

The Victim

For teenagers who have become the targets of various types of abuse, the nature of the attack may be physical or emotional, and the source may be peers, parents, or other adults. The type of child whom I call the Victim may suffer deep inner wounds that can often be healed only through extensive therapy.

Some signs that you may be the parent of an abused child:

- The youngster is often the target of verbal belittling or physical attacks at school or in the neighborhood.
- He tends to fall into the role of Victim by failing to assert himself in appropriate situations.
- She always follows other children, never acts as leader or displays independence.
- Your teenager will usually do what other children tell him to do.
- He seems scared or wary when around another adult.
- You have some evidence or strong suspicion that your child has been sexually abused.

• There are sometimes cuts, bruises, or other marks of violence on your child's body, other than the wear and tear that occur in sports or other activities.
• Your teenager seems depressed or unhappy much of the time.

To understand better how a child may become a Victim, let's explore in more detail three major types of abuse: peer abuse; emotional abuse by a parent; and sexual abuse by a parent or other adult.

THE PEER-ABUSE VICTIM

I've already told you that when I was both an elementary school student and an adolescent I was often pushed around and beaten up by classmates. In short, I was a peer-abuse Victim.

Another boy who had a related type of experience was fifteen-year-old Edward, who matured later sexually than most of his classmates. Instead of taking showers after physical education class or some sports event, he would hurriedly dress by crowding almost inside his locker and then go home by himself and take his bath in privacy.

Several of the other boys noticed Edward's modesty, and like many adolescents who try to build themselves up by tearing someone else down, they formulated a plan to embarrass him. Edward happened to be a fast runner, and so he decided to try out for the track team after school one day. After the workout, the other boys struck: They ganged up on him, pulled him down to the floor naked, and made fun of his lack of pubic hair.

This experience crushed Edward, who refused to go to the next track workout, even though he had made the team cut. At first, he wouldn't tell his parents what had happened. He just said, "I've decided I don't want to be on that team. I have too much schoolwork."

But that explanation didn't ring true with either his mother or father. Although they realized that they couldn't force their son to tell them what had happened, they weren't willing to give up on this issue, because they believed that the track team would be a good experience for him. So they began a concerted effort to break through and find out what the problem was.

First, they identified a time when he was most likely to open up to them. From past experience, they knew the best possibility was late in the evening, when he was ready for bed. As a child, he had always been inclined to talk about intimate matters when one of his parents was tucking him into bed, and that habit had persisted in a modified form into his teen years.

Then, the parents decided that his father should be the one to broach the subject of the track team. Many times, his mother was the first to hear about many of his deepest problems. But he and his dad were close too, and the parents sensed that on this issue the father might be the best person to explore the problem.

When Edward was in bed and had turned the light out, his father came into the room, pulled up a chair, and gently but directly raised the issue: "What about this track team business? What's the real problem?"

That was all it took. The frustration, embarrassment, and anger poured out of the boy. The father listened sympathetically and shared a similar experience that he had suffered through as a youth. "But I found I couldn't let those kids get me down," the father said. "If I had done that, I wouldn't have been in control of my life—*they* would have been."

In the ensuing discussion, Edward finally came to the conclusion on his own that he should try again with the track squad. "But how do I handle those guys?"

Both father and son agreed that at this point, it was best for him to try to take care of the matter himself rather than seek help from a coach. So they came up with this general plan:

- As difficult as it was for him, Edward would begin to take showers with the other team members. The boy and father agreed that was the only way he would have a chance to truly become an accepted member of the squad.

- He would develop some verbal comebacks when the inevitable razzing and belittling occurred in the locker room and showers. These didn't have to be worthy of a comedy slot on the *Tonight Show*. But he and his father tried to make them sufficiently incisive to disconcert the opposition.

- He would focus on becoming the best runner at his distance on the squad. The more accomplished he could become at the sport, the more accepted he would be by most of the teammates.

  "But I expect that some of the boys who were giving you trouble are also jealous of your speed," his father said. "By making fun of you, they hope to get rid of a tough competitor."

- He would make it a point to socialize with as many teammates as possible. The friendships he developed this way would work in his favor as he tried to gain general acceptance on the team.

As it turned out, this scheme worked better than either father or son had hoped. The very fact that Edward had the courage to go to track practice the next day, take a shower with everyone else—and run the legs off two of the boys who had abused him—immediately made him some friends among the other team members. Almost instantaneously, the overt victimizing stopped.

Although this result was the main objective of Edward and his parents, an equally important consequence was the enhanced communication in the family. Edward drew closer than ever to his father, because he saw in his parent an invaluable source of support and advice when the going got tough during adolescence.

THE EMOTIONAL-ABUSE VICTIM

I sometimes refer to physical abuse, such as beating on a kid with fists, as "blue-collar abuse," while emotional abuse might be termed "upscale abuse."

Obviously, the lines between these two types of victimizing aren't hard and fast. Sometimes, physical abuse may occur in the better educated, wealthier families, and emotional abuse can take place among those less well-heeled. But in general, emotional abuse seems to be a special problem for parents who would never consider raising a hand to their child.

One of the most serious kinds of emotional abuse occurs when a parent in effect tells a child, "You're no good. You're inadequate. You don't measure up."

This message can be communicated either verbally or through actions. One mother, for instance, was determined that her twelve-year-old daughter would be a great gymnast. All the girl's outside activities and many of the family weekends were devoted to practice sessions and out-of-town meets.

The problem wasn't so much the intensity of the training, but rather, the attitude of the mother. She constantly harped on the girl's mistakes and imperfections. When she would enter a meet and fail to place in the final standings, the mother would give her the silent treatment on the ride home and well into the evening. The message: "You have to perform well on those bars and mats for me to love you and accept you. Otherwise, you're just dirt."

The experience became extremely painful and nerve-racking for the girl, until finally she began to break down emotionally. She was constantly depressed and unhappy, and frequently cried, even though there seemed no particular reason to be unhappy.

Finally, a therapist was able to get to the bottom of the problem. He determined what was obvious to many friends of the family: that the mother was brutalizing the girl emotionally.

Although the process of correcting the situation was painful, the mother agreed to allow the girl to quit the sport. For a few weeks, the mother grieved over the loss of the activity, as one might grieve over the death of a loved one. Eventually, though, the dramatic change in her daughter's attitude toward life helped the mother begin to recover from her obsession with the sport. Then, the mother began to relate to her daughter more as a real person than as a gymnastics project.

Emotional abuse such as this can be a subtle force that can creep up on a family and drive wedges between parents and children. It's often hard to identify and correct because there can be a fine line between providing your child with plenty of opportunities to develop special talents, and pushing too hard for a "payoff" of high achievement. The challenge is for the parent to put her own agenda aside and place the teenager's needs at the fore.

THE SEXUAL-ABUSE VICTIM

Although physical abuse such as beatings is a terrible thing, sexual violations may be even more devastating emotionally *and* may be much harder to detect. In all types of abuse, and especially sexual abuse, it's important for the parent to trust his or her intuition and to act before matters get worse.

In this regard, I recall the situation faced by a seventeen-year-old girl who was sexually molested by her older brother over a period of years. Unfortunately, the father was away from home frequently on business trips and remained oblivious to the situation. The mother, though present, couldn't accept what was clearly going on before her eyes. She just denied that there was any problem.

The saddest part of this family tragedy was that the girl actually told her mother what was happening to her, and the mother did nothing about it. For that matter, the mother said she didn't even remember the conversation with her daughter!

During a counseling session, the girl related, "I can still remember exactly where we were when I told my mother. Where we sat, how scared I was."

When the mother failed to take action to stop the abuse, the girl began to assume that she and her father really didn't care for her that much. "Or I thought maybe this situation wasn't as bad as I thought. After all, if it was really so terrible, wouldn't my own parents do something about it?"

So the abuse continued until the girl was almost ready to graduate from high school. At this point, she shared the horror with a therapist she had been seeing, and she got immediate confirmation of what she had suspected all along: This sexual abuse by her brother was wrong and had to be stopped immediately.

Perhaps the most important consideration for parents who are informed about the sexual abuse of a child is to confront it right away for what it is. The problem shouldn't be sugar-coated and the resolution of it must not be postponed. Time is of the essence. The impact of sexual abuse caught at an early stage can often be mitigated by placing the child in a safer environment and making sure she knows she is loved and accepted, no matter what has happened to her. But years of sexual abuse can leave emotional scars that may never be completely eradicated.

Above all, don't deny! There's a temptation for parents who discover such abuse to try to sweep the problem under the rug. But when that happens, neither the child nor the family may ever recover.

Always remember, then, that time is all-important to a teenage Victim. The shorter the period of abuse—whether peer-induced, emotional, or sexual—the greater the odds that significant inner healing can be achieved.

CHAPTER 15

Toward a Mature Talking Relationship

The ten Kid Types that we've just discussed are *not* intended to be the Gospel According to Michael DeSisto. Rather, they're just meant to be an introduction to get you thinking. You need to be asking yourself, "Exactly what kind of teenager is living in my own home—and how can I get some good conversations started?"

Perhaps you've found that one or more of the kinds of kids I've described fit your son or daughter. On the other hand, you may also have felt compelled to alter, fine-tune, or even completely discard my suggestions in favor of an entirely new concept. And that's just fine. My only purpose has been to encourage you to think creatively about what kind of child you have and what his precise needs are. When you are able to engage in this kind of reflection, you'll be well on your way to understanding your youngster better and talking with him more meaningfully.

Ultimately, your main objective as the parent of an adolescent should be to help that young person negotiate successfully the transition from childhood to adulthood. You want him to emerge from the teen years with as little negative emotional baggage as possible. Also, you hope to help him realize his full potential as a special individual, one who will eventually be able to relate to you as a mature adult.

The stresses and strains of rearing a teenager are not the end of parenthood! The full joy of being a mother or father has yet to bloom in your home, my friend. Before long, the separation process will be complete. Then, that son or daughter will leave home permanently, establish a new family, and be ready to enjoy and nurture you on an adult-to-adult level. If you succeed in entering new and deeper levels of communication and interaction *now*, when your child is a teenager, the benefits can be tremendous when you're both adults.

What are some of those benefits? In encounters between parents and *adult* children, the Seven Secrets of Successful Communication that we discussed back in Chapter Four can take on a new and fuller meaning. Here's a sampling of what I mean:

Secret #1

Each family member will *continue* to have a "job description" —but the nature of those jobs will almost always change in exciting and constructive ways if the parent-teenager relationship has been rewarding.

For example, a son or daughter may be present as never before as an emotional and physical support for an aging parent. I'm not necessarily suggesting that your child will take care of you financially in your old age. In fact, I'd strongly suggest that you do everything you can to stay in control of your life and be self-supporting. It's always better for adult relationships if all concerned can remain relatively independent and work to minimize the financial and emotional burdens that others must bear.

On the other hand, intimacy between parent and teenager will usually carry over to adulthood in some fashion, and that usually means the continuation and intensification of trust, loyalty, and love. One son may take over the management of finances of his widowed mother. A daughter may monitor closely her physical health and arrange for her care if she becomes incapacitated. Still another son may be the one who takes her on most of her vacations.

When parent-child relationships have been placed on a healthy footing from the beginning, children and parents will find it much easier to relate in later life as adults. Furthermore, the lines of communication established when the children were teenagers will become even stronger. Yet the specific manifestations of the adult child's love will usually change, sometimes quite dramatically.

Secret #2

The games of the teenage years, such as red rover and pick-up-sticks, will also continue, but in altered form.

The point behind the red rover concept was to recognize that while conflict is bound to occur, it should be experienced on relatively safe battlegrounds. For example, you'll recall I recommended that when parents and teens fight, it's best to have at it on issues like clothing or caffeine consumption, not dangerous sex or drugs.

If the red rover game has been played properly during the adolescent phase, it's more likely that even though the parent and adult child may continue to quarrel occasionally, the issues will not threaten the relationship. A mother may chide a son for his failure to call or visit, for instance, but she won't threaten to cut off their relationship because she doesn't like the woman he's married.

Similarly, you may remember that in my version of pick-up

sticks, I discouraged attaching blame for difficult situations or pressures that arise in the family. The same applies when teenagers grow up. The best adult parent-child relationships are those where the finger of blame is rarely if ever pointed at anyone.

Secret #3

I recommended here that parents become experts at the "power play"—or empowering the youngster so that he can become more independent and responsible.

The adult child who has learned the proper uses of power at an early age can be a joy and support to his parents. The reason: He'll have the capacity to make tough decisions and take the initiative for life on his own.

In contrast, adult children who are overly dependent may constantly look to parents for advice and direction, and as a result, will never fully grow up. Sons and daughters in this state typically are incapable of responding effectively if at some point, a spouse, a family friend, or even the parent is in need of serious help.

Secret #4

I said that courage is the key to parent-child combat, and courage *continues* to be a key quality for successful family interactions in adulthood.

Parents of teenagers must have the guts to say "Stop it!" or, "No, that's wrong!" Otherwise, the children will never know what their limits are or where the lines of appropriate behavior should be drawn.

Similarly, both parents and adult children must have the inner strength to speak out clearly on issues where they disagree or where they have strong opinions. If an elderly father is about to blow part of his retirement savings on a harebrained investment scheme, the son or daughter shouldn't say, as one forty-year-old child did, "Well, it's his money, and he'll just learn the hard way." That's irresponsible and cowardly.

On the other hand, those kids who have been taught the virtues of courage by parental role models are more likely to take a stand later, when it really counts. In short, then, courage cuts both ways when teenagers grow up.

Secret #5

Teenagers must learn from their parents to avoid the Sieve Syndrome, which involves an inability to love, accept, and enjoy oneself.

Understanding this important lesson will greatly strengthen the young person for effective adulthood. There's nothing more annoying to many people than to have an acquaintance who is constantly looking for acceptance and approval, yet seems unable to receive the stroking that is offered. I know a number of older parents who rue those long-lost days when they failed to teach a child that he was a good person, entitled to celebrate his successes and triumphs.

"I'm *still* telling that boy he's a fine, competent, smart person, and he *still* doesn't seem like he believes me!" one eighty-one-year-old mother said of her fifty-eight-year-old son.

I mentioned the Sieve Syndrome to her, but I have a feeling my advice was coming a little late.

Secret #6

As you know, I believe strongly that fathers can have an invaluable emotional impact on sons, and likewise, understanding mothers are essential in the upbringing of daughters. When a parent of the same sex is absent because of death, divorce, or neglect, a suitable substitute of some type should be found.

I lacked a father during my teenage years because of his death when I was eleven, and I suffered for this. Perhaps if my dad had lived, I would have had a strong guide to help me make it more successfully through the Victim phase of adolescence, when I was the target of bullies.

Those children who are lucky enough to have living, nurturing, same-sex parents after they reach adulthood are lucky indeed. In these families, there's a special connection, a blood tie that can't be perfectly duplicated any other way.

On the other hand, I'm a great believer in the acquisition of *mentors* for those without parents, or those with partially or totally inadequate parents. By mentor, I mean an older person of the same sex who can act as a guide or companion during part or much of adulthood and can serve as a kind of surrogate parent. Many business leaders, accomplished educators, and other successful individuals have found that the mentors who took an interest in them have been perhaps the most important single factor in their achievements and emotional stability and perspective.

Secret #7

Finally, I recommended that parents celebrate their own shortcomings—because parental pathologies or mistakes often help kids to be stronger than would otherwise be possible.

The flaws of mothers and fathers may fade with age, but no parent can ever expect to become perfect. Yet, every parent can relax in the confidence that every *other* parent, since the beginning of time, has blown it in some fashion! So when your teenager leaves home, it's not helpful to constantly look back over your shoulder and moan, "Oh, if I had only done this or that!"

Perhaps you *should* have done something differently. But when you're dealing with an adult child, that's no time to become steeped in self-recriminations or wallow in guilt for the might-have-beens of parenthood.

Rather, the later years are a time to savor what you've done right, to offer additional help and support when you can, and to look to the future of your relationship with your grown kids. And if you've truly learned the special "code" that characterizes your teenager, what marvelous conversations the two of you will enjoy as you grow older together!

INDEX